MISS MANNERS
ON PAINFULLY PROPER WEDDINGS

OTHER BOOKS BY JUDITH MARTIN

*Miss Manners' Guide for the
Turn-of-the-Millennium*

Miss Manners' Guide to Rearing Perfect Children

*Miss Manners' Guide to
Excruciatingly Correct Behavior*

Common Courtesy

Style and Substance

Gilbert: A Comedy of Manners

Miss Manners®

ON PAINFULLY PROPER WEDDINGS

JUDITH MARTIN

Illustrated by Gloria Kamen

CROWN PUBLISHERS, INC.   NEW YORK

Copyright © 1995 by Judith Martin

Published by Crown Publishers, Inc., 201 East 50th Street,
New York, New York 10022. Member of the Crown
Publishing Group.

CROWN is a trademark of Crown Publishers, Inc.

Random House, Inc. New York, Toronto, London, Sydney,
Auckland

Manufactured in the United States of America
Library of Congress Cataloging-in-Publication Data

Martin, Judith
Miss Manners on painfully proper weddings :
/ Judith Martin . —1st ed.
p.   cm.
Includes index.
1. Wedding etiquette.   2. Weddings—Planning.   I. Title.
BJ2051.M37   1996   95-528
394'.22—dc20   CIP
ISBN 0-517-70187-1

10 9 8 7 6 5 4 3 2 1

First Edition

For Robert

Miss Manners

Thank you letters:

David Hendin
Ann Hughey

Miss Manners has no trouble writing thank you letters because her heart is overflowing with gratitude for her people agent and her wonderful assistants. However, those who have less cause to be grateful must still write gracious thank you letters for their ugly wedding presents.

CONTENTS

Contents

MISS MANNERS

ON PAINFULLY PROPER WEDDINGS

The Processional

Precision marching is less important for the bridal party than maintaining the proper facial expressions: The bridegroom must look awed; the bridesmaids, happy and excited; the father of the bride, proud; and the bride, demure. If the bridegroom feels doubtful, the bridesmaids, sulky, the father, worried, and the bride, blasé, nobody wants to know.

1

THE
GENERAL PRINCIPLES

This book is not supposed to be for brides. They are already reading far too many exhortations to pursue that cruelly elusive goal, earthly perfection.

Efforts to produce The Perfect Wedding have turned many a perfectly lovely bride into a perfect nuisance to her family, friends, and fiancé. One could hardly have a worse prelude to marriage than this notion that one can create one's own idea of perfection through controlling other people and conditions, even for a single day. Anyway, no bride in her right mind, if nature could produce such a wondrous creature, would want her wedding to be The Happiest Day of My Life. This would mean that everything from then on, such as the marriage itself, would be downhill.

With the kindest of wishes, Miss Manners suggests that the bride relinquish this book to others, go put her feet up, and have a nice, fragrant cup of tea.

Oh, all right, dear, here is one last checklist—Miss Manners knows that busy brides are hysterically attached to checklists—but one that is designed to cut down the bride's burden. It is called:

Things a Bride Need Not Trouble Her Pretty Head About

1. Do not worry about who is going to give you a shower. The shower is a lighthearted, nonessential element of an engagement (as opposed to, say, the fiancé, who is essential and whose heart should be fixed at this point). In any case, it is voluntary on the part of the bride's friends. They either throw one or they don't, but she can't demand one.

2. Do not worry about whether or not you like your relatives. You have to invite them anyway.

3. Do not worry about how many guests you can invite and still afford to serve your dream menu. The proper formula is to count up the relatives and friends first, and then figure out what you can afford to serve to that number of people.

4. Do not worry about whether people will give you wedding presents that you like. These are presents, after all, not fees paid for the privilege of seeing you get married. Only if guests ask what you want can you reluctantly admit to a preference for a certain style or category (which must include modest things), or to being registered at stores.

5. Do not worry about finding other ways to recoup some of the money spent on your wedding from your guests. You cannot do it.

6. Do not worry about whether the postage stamp on your invitations carries out the color scheme of your wedding. Nobody cares.

7. Do not worry, before you send out the invitations, whether or not the people you invite to your wedding will be able to get there. That's up to them to decide, once you send them the invitation. Later on, you can worry when they don't answer.

8. Do not worry about whether your bridesmaids will match one another, or whether there are the same number of them as there are groomsmen. This is not a parade or a public matchmaking. The idea is to have your friends around you, regardless of whether or not the effect is symmetrical. The attempt to form auxiliary couples for a wedding recessional has driven the affianced crazy with demands of "Well, I have to have Chris, so you've just got to find somebody else." Not only is there nothing wrong with having pairs of bridesmaids march together at the recessional, but no one is watching by then because their eyes are still misty from sentiment at the ceremony itself, or because they are looking around for their gloves now that the wedding is over.

9. Do not worry about whether your mother will match the bridegroom's mother. They are not a set, either, and can both be trusted to dress properly for the occasion.

10. Do not worry whether every minute of the wedding day will be captured on every electronic means available. It can ruin the occasion, and your friends will not long allow you to make yourself tedious by showing them pictures and videos.

11. Do not worry about "limousine" (there is no polite word for distinguishing pretentious automobiles from ordinary ones) privileges, pew seating, or dancing order. Aside from the general ideas that it is nice for people who are feeble or who are wearing long delicate dresses to get rides, that family watches the ceremony from up front, and that the bridal couple opens the dancing, there are no persnickety rules doling out the honors.

12. Do not worry about whether you have completed all your place settings. The stores will still be open after the wedding. Anyway, a proper bride is too busy writing thank-you letters in the first few months of marriage to put everything away.

13. Do not worry about whether the bridegroom is sufficiently interested in the wedding. He may or may not be, but this is not indicative of whether or not he loves you and whether or not he is ambivalent about getting married. The earliest you would ever need to consult him about such matters again is a whole generation from now, and Miss Manners assures you that your daughter will not be all that interested in whether her father thinks the wedding cake should be vanilla or chocolate.

The Bridegroom's Jurisdiction

DEAR MISS MANNERS—My sister's fiancé feels he needs to know everything about the wedding plans and have the say-so as to whether it should be done that way or not, even down to where the bridesmaids' dresses will be purchased, what style and color. He even wishes to be present when such choices are made. What exactly is the jurisdiction of the groom-to-be in planning a wedding? By the way, the wedding will be paid for by the bride's parents and each bridesmaid will pay for her dress.

GENTLE READER—Some time during the usual engage-ment, a tearful young lady clutching swatches of material goes to pieces and asks her fiancé, "What do you mean, that either the pink or the peach bows are okay with you? Don't you even care about your own wedding?" But as your indig-nation shows, and wise old Miss Manners knew all along, the idea that the wedding is of equal interest to both parties getting married is pretty much a polite fiction. The point is not who pays for it: The father of the bride would be simi-larly attacked by the mother of the bride if she hadn't been married long enough to know better. No form of egalitari-anism wipes out the fact that ladies are ordinarily more interested in the details of ladies' dresses than gentlemen are.

Nevertheless, it is the gentleman's wedding, also, and the right to participate in the planning is his if he wishes to claim it. You should be rejoicing for your sister. For the rest of her life, she will be the envy, when she shops, of ladies whose husbands have dropped them off and run, while hers sits backward on a little gilt chair and helps her choose her clothes.

A Lawyer's Warning

DEAR MISS MANNERS—As a divorce attorney, it seems to me that oftentimes it is the couples who were most lavishly and ostentatiously married who are most likely to get divorced. This seems even more true when the parents footed the wedding bill for the children. Indeed, I suspect a strong connection: Those "children" who demand expensive weddings from others are least likely to have the level of responsibility and maturity needed for a successful marriage. I would like to suggest a new set of wedding traditions, the loud protests of the Bridal Industry notwithstanding. How about this:

1. The young couple will pay for their own wedding. If they cannot afford even this, they certainly cannot afford a home, children, and the other usual accoutrements of marriage. Perhaps they should wait (as we did in the olden days) until they are a little better established.

2. The wedding will be paid for out of current income or assets. No one will borrow one cent to "put on" a wedding. If that means a small ceremony followed by luncheon at home, rather than The Dinner Dance of the Century, so be it.

3. No one else will be asked or expected to contribute to the pageant. It will not be some friend's or relative's expected "responsibility" to provide a shower, wedding breakfast, rehearsal dinner, etc. If you can't afford it, don't buy it.

4. No one will wear anything that they can't wear again. This means no rented "penguin suits" for the men; no outrageously expensive purple bridesmaids' dresses with the dyed-to-match *peau de soie* pumps; no $400 flower-girl dress for a five-year-old who is immediately going to spill orange juice on it.

5. The wedding party, minister, and guests will be allowed to do whatever they are supposed to do within the ceremony, and then to enjoy whatever celebration may follow without being constantly stopped, posed, and required to smile for one or more cameras so that the Pageant of the Century can be recorded for a century. Statistically, half of these photos are going to wind up on the cutting-room floor when the two young stars divorce, anyway.

6. The ceremony itself will be short, simple, and will wed the parties. Weddings are not an appropriate place to proselytize for one's religion, lecture the bridal couple or assembled guests on the duties of a good Jewish husband or Christian wife, or provide family members with a captive audience for their musical talents.

7. Serve soft drinks and spend what you would otherwise have spent on the liquor bill, on a down payment for the house.

8. Guests will refrain from sexual innuendoes and from comments about a bride's known or suspected pregnancy. That kind of ill-disguised envy and malice, or simple boorishness, is grounds for immediate expulsion of the offender.

9. Brides will accept and acknowledge each gift with graciousness and gratitude. They will recognize that due to a variety of reasons, not all gifts will be "new" or returnable, and they will never ask for a sales slip or suggest that they will exchange any gift, unless the giver makes the offer. (One-of-a-kind items,

such as handmade gifts or artwork or heir-looms, will simply have to be stored in the hope that one's children may like them.)

Guests, conversely, will recognize that their choice of gift may well be a duplicate or in the wrong color or simply not to the taste of the bridal couple and will, where possible, say "I got this at _____ and will help you to return it if it doesn't fit in with your decorating scheme."

10. Finally, close it down no later than 10 P.M. The old folks will appreciate it, the young folks who want to carouse will go elsewhere to do so, and the bridal couple can start their honeymoon sober and unhindered by Wedding Exhaustion.

A Priest's Reply

DEAR MISS MANNERS—As a parish priest, I have come, over the years, to detest performing wedding ceremonies. I am bothered by many of the same factors as the lawyer who wrote to you, and I am saddened and angered by the hurt and waste that accompany so many weddings.

But I quit cheering when I got to his sixth suggestion. More than anything, I resent being used to perform a service for a couple interested only in the romantic aura and clearly impatient with the religious elements of the ceremony.

By training and my own interest, I am intensely involved in many of the most important moments of people's lives. I see marriage as a gift from God, both to the individuals marrying, and to the society in which they live. When I conduct a service in which two people make a public commitment to each other, it is with the conviction that God had a part in making this marriage happen, and will have a part in keeping it together. The wedding is a religious rite, in my case a Christian rite, and I feel prostituted when I am asked to perform a wedding on any other basis.

Those who do not want to hear a religious perspective on what marriage is should ask a public official to conduct it. A pastor, priest, or rabbi is also the official of a religious organization that sees marriage within a religious context.

A Photographer's Lament

The mania for recording special moments on film and tape, rather than in the good old-fashioned memory, has eluded Miss Manners. That this should justify disrupting a religious service particularly offends her, and she has called upon the clergy to take a stand for dignity. Yet Miss Manners occasionally makes a pretense of being fair, and will now present and discuss the photographers' side.

"I try hard to be discreet during the ceremony," reports one photographer. "I never roam around the sanctuary, and I photograph without using a flash.

"I am under the direction of the wedding couple as far as what I do during the ceremony. I have been directed on occasion that they want specific shots taken with a flash during the nuptials, such as giving roses to their parents, or an overall shot from the balcony.

"To say that taking photographs during the ceremony should be banned is ridding the bride and groom of memorable shots of the actual ceremony with all the guests watching. Some of these shots just cannot be staged. If you had to stage all the shots of the ceremony, it would literally take at least two hours after the reception line. The same people who are complaining about the photographer during the wedding would be complaining about how long it is taking for the wedding couple to get to the reception so they can eat.

"The photographs I take during the wedding are very important to the couple, and they are paying to have them done. The privileged people who have been invited to share this moment as guests should realize this, and not be rude by talking negatively about how the couple choose to perform their ceremony."

The president of a photographers' association advances even a more solemn argument: "For hundreds of years, images and statues of religious figures have been used by the churches to help people relate to their God. Wedding photographs will serve to remind the bride and groom not only of the promises they made to each other, but to God as well. A professional photographer can easily photograph a wedding while preserving the dignity and sanctity of the service."

Predictably, Miss Manners does not succumb to the argument that the price of the service demonstrates its importance, or that guests should understand that they have actually been invited to a filming. She has yet to hear of a marriage's being saved because God had photographic evidence of the vows, and hopes that the idea of an instant replay of a wedding for the camera, while the guests are left to fend for themselves, is a joke.

However, certain points made by the photographers have riveted her attention. First, that it is possible to make quality photographs from discreet positions, and without use of a flash. Second, that it is the bridal couple, not the photographer, who bears the responsibility.

As bridal couples are often not in the most judicious of states, Miss Manners is all the more glad that she appealed to the clergy to set the standards. It seems that many of them do. Rules include restricting photographs to the processional and recessional, banning flash cameras, allowing only one photographer, or requiring video cameras to remain stationary. Some make announcements at the beginning of the ceremony, or on wedding programs, but others feel that setting conditions for having the ceremony there, and repeating the rules at the wedding rehearsal, suffice. "If couples ask for more leeway than we can accommodate," writes one pastor, "they are reminded that they might direct their attention to the sacred moment rather than becoming preoccupied with memories to enjoy later."

Is That Big Wedding Necessary?

An increasing number of couples are said to be eloping because they can't bear going through the ordeal of a conventional wedding. Far from disapproving, Miss Manners would be suspicious of anyone planning a big wedding who didn't sigh at least once about how much nicer it would be to elope. Someone so seduced by the envisioned glory of the occasion as to fail to remark, "Darling, don't you just wish the two of us could slip away without all this fuss?" (not necessarily putting down the three-ring notebook with the telephone numbers of florists and bands) probably shouldn't be getting married.

Yet Miss Manners would also like to caution against impetuous elopement, and not only because wily caterers have come to require a deposit. Avoiding fuss is something she can understand. So let's talk fuss.

In some cases, it is the competing desires of relatives and friends that are thought to create too much fuss. Families want the wedding held in one place, friends in another; the bride and bridegroom come from different cultural or religious backgrounds, perhaps from more than one each; the older generation's idea of festivity is different from the younger's; and everyone seems to have enemies among those who ought to be invited.

This situation strikes Miss Manners as an excellent opportunity for the couple to learn how to placate others and negotiate compromise, surely requirements for family life. Elopement is merely the kind solution to avoid all-out warfare between irreconcilable factions (which means something more than the couple's wanting a rock band and the parents' wanting old show tunes) and lasting animosities that would obliterate the fact that marriage is the joining of two families.

The fuss that others want to avoid is the time and energy, not to mention money, involved in putting on a lavish production. They are quite right. Running a three-day show for hordes of business acquaintances is neither necessary nor tasteful.

What does seem to be necessary to the human spirit is some sense of ritual connected with so momentous a step in life. It amuses Miss Manners that people who have talked about getting married for years, and very likely already share a household, are deeply interested in the rituals of the formal wedding. It touches her, too. Presumably there are people who never regret having skipped any semblance of ceremony when they married. But Miss Manners keeps hearing from those who made the decision to marry without any fanfare and are now complaining that they missed out on an entitlement and asking how to make up for it.

Miss Manners seems to have missed the section of the Constitution that guarantees every couple an elaborate wedding. A proper wedding is simply a dignified ceremony, followed by a celebration for those who care about the couple, in a more formal version of the way they usually entertain. It also seems to her that those who married without ritual are free to have post-wedding receptions and then anniversary parties that are as elaborate as they like, but should not feel that the world has cheated them.

What is marriage, if not the ability to make a decision and then stick by it later?

Family Wishes

DEAR MISS MANNERS—Believe it or not, I have no desire for a big, traditional wedding. My dream is to elope while on vacation, getting married on a tropical beach. No hassles, no outlandish costs, no pomp and circumstance. How do I handle family and friends who would expect the traditional wedding? Mom, my best friend, would be devastated (I think). I'm the only daughter. What sort of after-event could we have to share our joy with everyone? Is there elopement etiquette?

GENTLE READER—The traditional reason for an elopement was to thwart the hopes, plans, and dreams of the bride's parents, which is why the entire rest of the world sympathized with elopers. Thwarting parents has always had a wide sentimental appeal, even among people who don't know the parents or anyone else concerned.

It is also why the traditional elopement was sometimes followed by the traditional annulment. When the mean and unromantic parents pointed out that the bride was supposed to be in junior high school and the bridegroom was wanted in four states, happily ever after could be prematurely terminated. But even now, when parents are considerably less vigilant, couples elope. They could be eluding mean and unromantic employers with an antinepotism policy.

There are many reasons for an elopement, some of them nicer than others. Perhaps the couple wishes to spare their parents (or themselves) the expense. Or they have been married before and wish to spare others the fuss that may have been made over one or both of them on previous marriages. Perhaps they are thwarting parents in a modernized way—eluding parental ideas of a proper wedding, rather than parental ideas of the proper spouse. Or they consider that the choice of wedding scenery is more important to them than the people who would otherwise be the wedding guests.

Miss Manners has no desire to talk people into big weddings, pomp and circumstance usually being more threatening than encouraging to proper wedding behavior. But pray, what do you call a hassle if it is not causing devastation for your mother (and thus, as you gracefully say, also for your best friend)? That you may be satisfied with a vacation wedding is not enough if it would cause genuine distress to your mother.

That is not to say others cannot be talked around. If your mother would be satisfied with a big wedding reception upon your return from elopement, Miss Manners certainly has no objection.

Is That Second Big Wedding Necessary?

DEAR MISS MANNERS—Please inform us how etiquette applies to the bride's second wedding. When my daughter was married five years ago, the marriage lasted two years and ended in divorce. She has been living for two years with another young man, and they are planning to be married. She wants a large church wedding, complete with white flowing wedding gown and veil and several bridesmaids.

At her first wedding, she received many, many beautiful gifts from our generous family, friends and business associates. She was well supplied with fine and casual china, silver and stainless flatware, and crystal in her chosen patterns.

She intends to select and register new patterns of silver, china, and crystal. I question the propriety, and am embarrassed that our family, friends and associates will feel pressured to give another nice gift.

GENTLE READER—Your daughter quarreled not only with her husband, but with her silverware? My, that is anger. Or did he manage to clean her out during the divorce?

No matter. Miss Manners is addressing her answer to the part about wedding presents to the guests, anyway. Since your daughter will of course only admit to being registered when she is specifically asked, it is they who need to decide whether they need help in figuring out what to give her. Wedding presents, particularly elaborate ones, are not as customary with subsequent weddings as with a first. There is nothing wrong with seeing someone married twice (or however long she plans to keep it up), and sending only a token present after the first time, or even just a letter wishing her well.

There is something wrong about inviting the same people to more than one splashy formal wedding, but people, even amazingly including Miss Manners, are inclined to be indulgent about violations. The truly proper second wedding is small and relatively informal—the bride wears a perfectly smashing suit, in a delicate pastel color rather than white, and an even more smashing hat instead of a veil. She has one honor attendant, not a parade of them, partly because all her old friends now know that her previous promise to them—never mind her promise to her previous bridegroom—was false. They have *not* had other occasions to wear those bridesmaid dresses she made them buy.

Before Miss Manners is attacked by starry-eyed brides who made one tiny little mistake and now want to go all out for what they insist is their first true marriage, notice that she is waving a tiny, white, lace-edged handkerchief. She is neither so vulgar as to associate the white dress with inexperience, nor so mean as to throw etiquette brickbats in place of rose petals.

Family Disapproval

DEAR MISS MANNERS—I am a 36-year-old woman who is living with a man of a different race. My elderly parents do not approve, but have managed, over time, to cloak their true feelings with a thin veneer of civility. Ed and I are soon to be married in a small civil ceremony and are looking forward to starting a family.

My very elderly godparents live out of state and I have kept them pretty much in the dark with the excuse that I didn't want to "upset" them. I am virtually certain that my parents haven't said anything to my other relatives. If I were suddenly to send an announcement of my marriage, they would all (rightly) wonder why they hadn't heard of Ed before; yet I don't feel a need to explain or justify myself. They will all be shocked and/or horrified by my choice of husband, and, though I abhor their racial prejudices, I wish to be as tactful as possible. My idea for handling the problem was to enclose a photo of us along with the wedding announcement.

GENTLE READER—Miss Manners approves of your approach, in neither challenging your relatives nor explaining your decision, and would only like to make one small suggestion about your solution. A formal wedding announcement out of the blue is, as you say, startling to close relatives. Write them individual letters instead—without referring to your previous silence, because suggesting that an explanation would have upset them is insulting to them, as well as to your husband-to-be.

In a letter, you can offer the usual bridal chitchat—that you and Ed have known each other for a long time, that he's the most wonderful man in the world, and so on—to make it seem that you are ready to include them in your circle should they respond more favorably than you predict. Adding the picture to a letter then becomes not a challenge, but a charming gesture.

In the Family Way

DEAR MISS MANNERS—My fiancé and I, who have been living together for over a year, set our wedding date six months ahead of time and announced it to our family and friends. We were planning a large church wedding with all the trimmings. Now I suspect that I may be pregnant, and by the wedding date I would definitely be showing. We would like to go forward with our plans regardless. Please advise as to what kind of wedding would be appropriate.

GENTLE READER—For the pregnant bride, a wedding is considered highly appropriate. The one thing Miss Manners believes should be altered is the wedding dress: Let it out in the tummy.

Fooling with Tradition

Can weddings be run without the factor of sex playing a significant part?

Oh, dear. That does not at all sound like what Miss Manners intended. What she means to discuss is whether the division of tasks and honors by gender, which has always characterized weddings, should be overhauled in the light of gender enlightenment. Some of the questions that keep arising are:

Why are the bride's parents' names, but not the bridegroom's parents', on the invitation?

> Why do they get to have the wedding in their hometown (question from bridegroom's parents)?
>
> Why do we get to pay for everything (question from bride's parents)?
>
> Why is it the bride's previous marital history, not the bridegroom's, that determines whether it is classified as a first wedding?
>
> Why are there domestic showers for brides, and hilarious drinking parties for bridegrooms?
>
> Why does she get given away while he just donates himself?
>
> Why do the attendants of each have to be the same gender as they are?
>
> Why does everyone look at her and no one at him?

Rather than await Miss Manners' pronouncements on these questions, many bridal couples have taken matters into their own hands, or sometimes fists. It is not uncommon now to see lots of parental names on invitations, to hear that the bride's friends took her out to a strip joint while the bridegroom's friends had a quiet dinner at a respectable restaurant, and for everyone concerned to claim that everyone else concerned (and some people who just happened to be briefly passing through the family) should contribute to paying the bill.

It is high time that Miss Manners made some order out of all this. She is not against change. Etiquette is continually evolving, and always has been, as life changes. Full dignity for ladies is one of the best changes to come along in centuries.

But tradition also has a claim; why else are all these hysterical people involved in putting on this spectacle?

Customs that have outlived their original reasons may nevertheless still carry emotional weight. Orderly change consists of adapting tradition to the actual situation it is to adorn. First, one must determine what is essential about the tradition, and what not—in this case, whether it is gender or some other factor that is important.

The bride's parents traditionally gave the wedding because she went from their house and support to her husband's. Their names alone were on the invitation because they were the hosts. It is the first wedding that makes the pomp attractive to guests who have not been through the emotions of watching this particular bride being married before. After that, although they may fervently hope for the best, they are not quite so starry-eyed about the "forever" ritual.

Certainly both sets of parents, or the bridegroom's alone, can give the wedding, or the bridal couple themselves or their friends. Parents' names may be retained as sentimental figureheads, even if the couple does all the planning.

What no one concerned can do is to assign bills to other people, and sell or withhold wedding honors. This being a family matter, not a business concern, financial contributions are volunteered, not mandated. One set of parents cannot be hosts, yet assume they can farm out bills to the other set. (However, among families and prospective families, any offers of help, especially if there is a need, are gracious, and qualify as strictly family business with which etiquette would not dream of interfering.)

Considering that brides seldom grow up next door to their bridegrooms, the identity of the latter becomes necessary in a way it never used to be. Miss Manners does not object to an invitation saying whose son he is, although she prefers that the bridegroom's parents merely slip a formal card with their names into invitations for their side of the list.

For the bride to be given away is another anachronism, more charming than necessary. If her mother brought her up alone, it should be she who gives the bride away, not a more distant male relative. The Jewish custom of having both sets of parents accompany their children is the most charming of all, provided we're not talking about melées between those parents and their marital successors.

Attendants are supposed to be the principals' closest friends and the gender division merely reflected segregated social lives. Friendship should outweigh gender as a factor in choosing attendants and Miss Manners is tired of being asked whether this requires cross-dressing. Ladies still dress as ladies, and they should still attract more attention from the wedding guests. Miss Manners is not saying that will never change, but it hasn't yet.

Playing the Fool

Nasty news from the bridal front reminds Miss Manners of the danger of letting people think for themselves. In the desire to get bridal couples to calm down and do some of their own planning to fit their own circumstances, she has recklessly implied that they should use their own judgment. Ever the optimistic believer in the human intelligence, she forgot to specify that judgment must include a sense of dignity.

It seems that joking at the altar has become commonplace enough for a justice of the peace to anticipate exactly what form it is going to take: The bridegroom will "play to the crowd, saying, 'Hmmm, I'll think about it' instead of 'I will,' or pretending to screw the bride's ring on if it proves difficult."

The ceremonial kiss is used as a public sample of the couple's love-making. "I try to remind both the bride and the groom that the kiss at the end of the ritual should be brief, as it is a token," reports the justice of the peace. "Yet I wish I could tell you of the grooms who 'swallow' their brides while the assembled guests clap to indicate their appreciation. The brides clutch their headpieces, bouquets, and anything else that is falling off during this display of 'love.' "

In an understandable desire to include their children ("his-hers-theirs," explains Miss Manners' informant while pleading "Not if they are under five!"), couples allow the ceremony to be undermined. "I am not referring to having them be bridal attendants, but to participating. I cannot 'marry' three people. If they want to hold their baby while I'm talking, so be it, but I don't think it makes the baby feel more wanted, as it is too young to appreciate the significance. It just points up to all assembled that the child was born out of wedlock. Putting little children in outlandish costumes they can't manage seems cruel."

It is a kindly meant innovation to have the bride and bridegroom's children present at the ceremony, on the grounds that they are becoming part of a new family. But Miss Manners worries that the tendency is to pressure the children into what amounts to a command performance, regardless of whatever emotional reservations they may have about committing to the stepparent or feeling that it is a betrayal of the absent parent. Children should have the choice of not attending and, at most, merely accompany the parent to the altar.

Then comes the reception: "Here is a mild toast from one of the many best men who has no idea of how to make a toast—'Here's to John and Mary and the little one!' Most guests did not know the bride was pregnant; her stricken face attested to that," he writes. "My favorite standard toast is 'Here's to you and here's to me, friends may we always be, but if we part, here's to me and to hell with you!' Isn't that a great toast for a wedding? How about this one (formal wedding, mind you)—'Here's to John and Mary, and all I can say is, it took a f——ing long time.'

"It is more and more prevalent for the couple to grind the wedding cake in each other's faces. Even fathers will urge the groom to 'give it to her, smoosh it in her face.' I've seen brides with cake in their cleavage, grooms with frosting on their moustaches and beards. Bear in mind that not all wedding cakes nowadays are white or yellow.

"DJs or bandleaders who think they are there to entertain have no sense of propriety. The man who caught the garter is importuned to put it 'higher, higher' on a girl who is squirming because she is modest, or has fat or skinny legs, or is wearing only knee-high hose with a long gown, and who is embarrassed at all that attention. I have seen a thirteen-year-old boy urged to put the garter on a thirty-year-old.

"People tinkle glasses incessantly, and with a vengeance, for the couple to kiss. Some get so vigorous that the stemware goes flying. At one formal wedding, the bride had provided little wooden mallets for the guests."

Miss Manners is also sadly aware that such travesties of the wedding ceremony and celebration are not isolated instances. The ancient history of wedding jokes does not prevent Miss Manners from noticing how revolting they are. The perpetrators fail to understand the difference between making an occasion enjoyable and making a significant event into a mockery. Some time ago, half suspecting it was a joke, she answered a query about a wedding in which the bridal party had decided to be nude; the mail has since brought several accounts of similar ventures.

However, if she withdraws delegating some judgment to bridal couples, she never will get back to the porch swing. Rather than saying you shouldn't use your own judgment in planning your wedding, she would like to suggest that you shouldn't be planning a wedding unless you have developed some judgment.

Oh, Stop

DEAR MISS MANNERS—At a wedding reception I attended, the bridegroom took off the bride's garter with his teeth. Is this considered inappropriate wedding etiquette? Is it considered appropriate or not for the bride to sit on the best man's lap while the groom takes off the bride's garter?

GENTLE READER—You know the answers, and the people doing these things don't care. So why spoil Miss Manners' day? It's times like this that make her wonder why she went into the etiquette trade instead of something easy, like teaching canaries to fetch sticks.

2

TERRIBLE IDEA I
The Wedding as "My Day"

That people should get married when they are old enough to know what they are doing seems to Miss Manners to be a remarkably good idea. She would think it reasonable to assume that by that time, they also know enough about themselves, their families, their friends, and human nature, and also about how to entertain, to be able to plan an event that brings all these people together in harmony and delight.

Not necessarily, it seems. Wisdom apparently often deserts even the most levelheaded people when it comes to their own weddings. Having presumably learned life's most important lesson—that other people have feelings that must be taken into consideration—they have been known to regress for this one event.

Never mind that maturity had a lot to do with making them desirable as marriage partners. With the modern form of extended courtship (extended beyond parental patience) there is ample opportunity to discover before marriage whether someone else is unselfish enough to take an interest in one's own happiness. It should therefore set off a warning when either one says (or hears), "Ever since I was small, I wanted . . ." or "This'll be a good

chance to . . ." or "After all, we're the people who are getting married, so . . ."

Only a warning. Miss Manners, who always assumes the
best, is ready to hear these openings properly completed:

"Ever since I was small, I wanted to marry someone
wonderful and kind."

"This'll be a good chance to gather all the people we
care about and show them how much they mean to us."

"After all, we're the people who are getting married, so
we should take the responsibility and see to it that this
doesn't unduly burden our parents."

Here, for any brides or bridegrooms who are old
enough to know better but may have forgotten, is a
reminder list of wedding wisdom.

1. Secret fantasies should remain fantasies, if not
   secret. No good will come of their being acted
   out in public. Miss Manners has heard from
   multidivorced grandmothers who confide that
   with their latest engagements they see an opportunity to hold the wedding of their childish
   dreams, designed for nubile brides shyly
   emerging from their parents' protection; and
   from successful businesswomen who never
   would have dreamed of going into show business but who now want to express themselves
   in wedding dramas of their own making. She
   sympathizes with both, provided they get a
   grip on themselves. Miss Manners believes all
   weddings should be festive, but one should
   not depend too heavily on the indulgence
   even close friends have for the showily inappropriate.

2. Parenthood is not exclusively a financial relationship and thus its privileges cannot be sus-

pended when the payments cease. Grown children cannot reappear demanding that they are owed sponsorship of their weddings, nor can they announce that they plan to ignore their parents' feelings and opinions on this family occasion, since they themselves are paying the bills.

3. While most people are pleased to hear that their friends or relatives are getting married, few are so moved as to want to mortgage their own futures in order to make all the couple's dreams come true. Anyway, it is the guests, not the bridal couple, who are supposed to come up with the idea of wedding presents.

4. Guests are guests, and must be treated hospitably even when the hosts happen to be using the day to get married. "We're only having foods we like" is the wrong attitude; the right one is, "We're having special treats that we think everyone will enjoy," even if this is applied to the same menu.

5. A wedding is not an opportunity to boss other people around, whether this means assigning bridesmaids to buy dresses they hate or divorced parents to behave as if they were still married. Neither, for that matter, is a marriage such an opportunity.

Planning "My Day"

DEAR MISS MANNERS—What about inviting people verbally, say five months before, and then changing your mind? I realize that it's not right, but sometimes in the expansive mood of the engagement, these mistakes are made. In addition, I've known some sourpusses for many years. They could easily pout their way through the wedding and not share the happiness. Yet I've known them for fifteen years or so, and feel an obligation (somewhat). How much of my day really is this wedding day, anyway?

GENTLE READER—You pushed the wrong button here. Miss Manners hates that bridal canard about My Day (even aside from the question of why isn't it Our Day?)—as if getting married, of all things, gave one the right to suspend normal consideration of others. Here you are contemplating using it to disinvite guests (which would be a high insult) or to rate your friends and relations on whether they will be able to produce suitable facial expressions (which would be a new low in choosing bridal accessories).

"My Day" Ever After

DEAR MISS MANNERS—At the time of my wedding, my fiancée/wife unfortunately decided to enforce her standards of aesthetics and insisted that one of my closest friends shave off a beard of dubious aesthetic value as a condition to be an usher.

I was unsuccessful in dissuading her from this course and, on the theory that a wedding day is the bride's day, I reluctantly backed her against my better judgment. My friend understandably chose to withdraw from the wedding party rather than be dictated to. I never was comfortable with the decision and regretted that I could see no middle course. What should/could I have done to avoid the damage to my friendship without alienating my bride?

A second instance involved a social gathering at which some fairly heated opinions were exchanged. My wife took, to my mind, a somewhat outlandish opinion and, when she seemed unable to persuade others, she turned to me for support—insisting on my unqualified support, although I did not agree with her. I tried to soft-pedal the disagreement with innocuous attempts—"Well, that's certainly an interesting viewpoint," or "You can certainly look at it that way," but it was to no avail. During the ride home, I was roundly criticized for my failure to rally unconditionally to her side.

I have to emphasize that my personal view was that her opinion was—ah—not in the mainstream of conventional thought. How could I better have handled this dilemma between intellectual honesty and personal commitment? I tried, I really did, but both situations blew up in my face despite my best efforts to avoid this.

GENTLE READER—Miss Manners seeks to avoid these problems by stamping out that appalling belief, to which even you subscribed out of kindness, that a wedding is "the bride's day," during which she is permitted to act as a tyrant.

It is, as you have discovered, an extremely bad precedent. Miss Manners can hardly think of anyone for whom consideration for the feelings of others is as crucial as someone who is getting married. It would be nice if your gentle attempts to avoid making stands that displease your wife resulted in her appreciation for your character and her desire to reciprocate. Unfortunately, such does not appear to have been the case.

Having been backed into dictating to your friend on a matter that concerns him alone—wedding attendants are supposed to be chosen for their friendship, not their beauty, and this wasn't even her wedding attendant but yours—the lady now believes that she can dictate your opinions. Miss Manners is afraid that you will have to disabuse her of this error if you are to have any hope of having a pleasant married life.

Marital loyalty is a wonderful thing, and Miss Manners does not wish to minimize the manifold opportunities to practice it. But professing opinions of which you disapprove is not such an instance. This is not just because it would violate your moral obligations to state your opinions honestly. Actually, marriage sometimes requires doing just that—for example, saying, "I thought you did great" or "You look wonderful." But marriage, as it involves two people with separate brains, does not require professing a unified intellectual stance (and hers, at that, with no consideration given to the possibility of its occasionally being yours).

The Berserk Bride

DEAR MISS MANNERS—One of my brothers is about to be married to a woman I liked very much when we met. Since then, however, I have become appalled.

I observed her and her friends doing the "white glove test" at a dinner party. She has asked my parents to pay half the wedding costs (her parents have encouraged her to reduce her expectations). She called my mother to ask exactly what her future in-laws will give as a wedding present and, when told, said, "Oh, I guess that will be okay." I have been making a quilt and, when the quilt top was done, she strongly desired that I make the two-hour round-trip for her to inspect it. Everything is done with a cheerful voice and pleasant smile, but it makes her behavior no more appealing. I wish to be polite, but my stress level increases with each encounter. The wedding is three months away!

GENTLE READER—Three months seems sufficient time for you, and perhaps your parents as well, to have a cozy little chat with your brother. It should go something like this:

"Tiffany is such a lovely girl, dear; we're all so happy for you. We're so much looking forward to having her in the family. I'm sure that she'll soon get used to our ways. But perhaps—since we don't want to get off on the wrong foot with her—you'd better tell her about us. As you know, we'd like you both to have lovely things, but we can't really see paying for a lavish wedding. And we felt funny about being asked about our presents. Tell her to have a little more faith in our desire to welcome her, even if she doesn't find us able to be as generous as you may have led her to expect. The quilt is a labor of love, but it's really not reasonable to make a special trip to have it inspected. Tell her I want her to be happy with it, but I just don't have that kind of leisure. Darling, I hope you didn't make her think we were rich, or had unlimited free time. But what we do have is lots of love to give your wife; see if you can make her understand that."

The Reasonable Bride

DEAR MISS MANNERS—As a bride-to-be, I've noticed a little bit of something resembling Open Season on Brides, even in your own lovely column. Brides all over are being chastised as being selfish, petty, insensitive, etc., these days.

In response, I'd like to make a few suggestions to the friends and family, and friends-and-family-in-law, of the bride-to-be:

1. Out-of-towners: No, I did not schedule my wedding on your birthday or anniversary just to annoy you. I picked it because it was the only day available in my church in the next calendar year. If you can't come, I'm sorry. If you do come, please don't complain to me about your accommodations, the food at the reception, or how much all this nonsense is costing you. I already know how much it costs. I'm helping to pay for it.

2. Close friends: Don't ask me "Why wasn't I asked to be a bridesmaid?" Please be careful not to rewrap and give me the gift I gave you for your wedding.

3. Attendants: If you can't afford the expense, tell me when I ask you to be an attendant. Then I can offer to pay, or you can bow out gracefully. If you said you want some say in how the dresses look, keep your eyes peeled and help me shop. Please keep in mind that I'm dealing with a group of women of very different tastes and sizes and I'd like to please you all as much as possible. When invited to "preview" a dress before the decision, either go and look at it and give me your opinion, or don't complain about the choice made. Please don't fuss about the relative size or attractiveness of the other ladies or the groomsmen. They're also my friends.

4. Groomsmen and best man: I spent months planning for this day. I would appreciate it if you would deliver the groom to the church on time, not noticeably suffering from the effects of too much alcohol.

5. In-towners: If you can stand the thought, offer to put up some out-of-towners. You will claim my undying devotion. Offers to drive these people to the reception, to the airport, or wherever will also be greatly appreciated. Some day I may be able to return the favor for your child.

6. Family: Talk about the "other" family quietly, preferably somewhere else, after the reception.

7. Everyone: Please answer my invitation promptly. And don't do it with a phone call, either. If you don't want to get me a present or throw me a party, fine. There's no obligation. Just don't try to explain it to me.

Please don't criticize my choice of china, crystal or silver—or husband. Don't ask me how much anything, or all of it, costs. Make an effort to socialize with anyone who looks lonely at the reception. Don't ask if you can bring a friend!

If you could make an attempt to do the above, I'd appreciate it more than all the presents or parties in the world. And please—no more spoiled-bride anecdotes. I may snap and run after you, screaming, waving my Bridal Organizer.

GENTLE READER—Miss Manners will thank you for this excellent lesson, just as soon as she can control the blush suffusing her delicate cheeks. For indeed, you are quite right that Miss Manners has allowed herself to become snappish during wedding season, when she has been overexposed to brides whose credo is After-All-It's-My-Day. Any sensible person who hears someone speaking in an imperious tone of "her day" would be wise to consider that it therefore isn't going to be anyone else's day, and to leave her to enjoy it alone.

To brides such as yourself, who try to plan a pleasant day for everyone, only to suffer the sort of treatment you describe, Miss Manners offers her apologies, sympathies, and pledge of assistance.

3

TERRIBLE IDEA II
The Wedding as Fund-raiser

When people used to speak of "marrying for money," it meant that one half of a bridal couple was plundering the other. Nobody, with the possible exception of the impoverished side of the aisle, considered that quite nice. But at least it kept whatever monetary exploitation was being practiced within the family—allowing for the fact that the family was actually being formed for that purpose.

Miss Manners has been told that brides and bridegrooms are not as inexperienced and innocent on their wedding days as they used to be. They have lawyers. But however much the possibility of greed between lovers may have been curbed by caution, the association of that nasty appetite in connection with matrimony does not seem to have been suppressed. Only now it is the guests to whom bridal couples turn when they think of making a profit out of matrimony. Marrying for money has come to mean making a profit from the wedding guests, through direct cash contributions and wedding presents, after deducting the expenses of allowing them to attend.

Ever the romantic, Miss Manners has never actually believed that expectation of toasters is what motivates people to get married. She is quite severe with those who assume that other people only get themselves born, graduated, married, and pregnant for the purpose of extracting presents from them. But her Ghastly Wedding File is unfortunately bulging with anecdotes suggesting that guests are no longer considered people with whom brides and bridegrooms wish to share their happiness without regard to the possibility that they may be moved to give some token of their pleasure at the event:

"The groom sent out an invitation by office computer, with a choice of entrees ($22 for steak, and $19 each for filet of sole or chicken Marsala), and the notations, 'No host cocktails,' 'Please R.s.v.p. with payment to ——' and 'There will be a money or gift basket available.' "

"We received a wedding invitation from a young couple being married in a black-tie affair at an exclusive club— '$150 per couple.' I have seen this for political fund-raisers, but never for a private celebration."

"I was invited to a wedding dinner in a restaurant, where the check was handed to the groom and without announcing the amount, he instructed everyone to pass down $75 a person. I did not drink any of the expensive wine, or coffee, and I split a dessert. The following day, I learned that my portion of the bill was less than $30 including tip."

"I have been informed that an invited guest gives a money gift based on the cost of the wedding reception. In other words, if it is a nice, sit-down dinner with an orchestra, the guest is expected to give at least $100. Is a wedding reception now a charity event or an evening out which guests pay for, like the parties I attended at college, where you gave $5 at the door to help the frat boys cut the cost of beer and snacks?"

"I would like your opinion of the growing number of 'Jack and Jill' parties, often organized by the engaged couple themselves, selling tickets for a dinner dance, and keeping the profits after expenses. Are these proper?"

"The father of the bride, my relative, has informed me that my wedding gift (a handmade, Native American work of art of museum quality) was not appropriate. While refusing to assign a value to the item, he said it was not right, meaning not adequate, in view of the fact that four members of my family will be in attendance."

"Just when I thought I'd seen it all, my daughter received a wedding invitation—not even from a close friend—with a card asking, 'If you would like to assist us in saving for the purchase of our first home together' and giving the name of their mortgage company. Thinking and hoping it was a joke, I called the 800 number. Sad to say, it's not."

"Under the R.s.v.p., there was listed a money amount per person, with the notation, 'Includes dinner, dancing, and gift.' Is it considered appropriate for the invited guests to pay for the festivities and to chip in for a gift to be determined by someone else?"

"A member of the bride's family passed a hat decorated with flowers and ribbons indicating it was for donations for the honeymoon. This is the second time this has happened to me. Is this the latest trend?"

In what one must presume to be an advance of delicacy, one couple offered a chart with a heart to be placed by the guest donor, indicating whether that person's contribution should be spent on such choices as "a night on the town," "a moonlight cruise," or "shopping for souvenirs." Another bride, eschewing the crudity of collecting cash, listed her demands with the catalog numbers from which they could be ordered.

It was Miss Manners's last illusion that people who engaged in such practices were aware that they had sacrificed any vestige of politeness, and were just too greedy to care. Then she got the following letter, not even from the person who stood to profit:

"Recently, I had a bridal shower for one of my girl-friends. I decided to have people send in $15 each for a group gift. This request was actually printed on the invitation. Now I know what is right, but I found that many people do not. Those who regretted did not send in their $15. I come from a middle-to upper-class society, and I was just shocked at this. I know what is socially correct, so this is not a question, rather a reminder to those in my circles who need a refresher course on their manners."

Miss Manners is relieved at the notation that this was not a question. It saves her picking herself up from the floor, where she fell into a dead heap at the death of decency and hospitality—never mind romance.

Financial Frankness

DEAR MISS MANNERS—A couple in their midthirties, who will be married next month, have registered at a large department store for various household goods and china. However, they have made it quite clear that they do not intend to keep the china, but return it for cash to be used to purchase a stereo system. I am appalled. I am in my mid-thirties, too—am I THAT old? Another bride, who has lived on her own for a few years, said that she wanted to have lots of showers so that she can get a lot of gifts. I just do not understand the greed. Money is not a problem for either couple, which is demonstrated by both brides purchasing expensive dresses and planning large receptions. Can you give me an explanation of what is going on?

GENTLE READER—Greed? You want Miss Manners to explain greed to you? And then what? Lust and sloth? Instead, she will modestly limit herself to explaining why greed, always part of the human condition, is now so frankly expressed, rather than decently concealed.

The appalling idea that openness is a virtue, regardless of the sin being flaunted, has been around for a generation or so now. That is why one hears ugly confessions accompanied by the self-righteous declaration, "But I'm not going to be a hypocrite," and why those who are timid about condemning dreadful behavior affect to be upset only by the transgressor's having subsequently lied about it.

In that spirit of total revelation, bridal couples are cheerfully admitting to their wedding guests that they are deeply focused on the presents they will receive and that, far from leaving the choice to the generosity and taste of their friends, they see the wedding as an opportunity to make others do their shopping for them.

Within this context, the couple willing to launder the money through some hapless store's china department may think themselves marvels of subtlety. Since they went and blabbed their scheme, Miss Manners can hardly agree with them. All this frankness is highly unflattering to the guests, of course. They might have harbored the notion that the couple, being primarily interested in their friendship, was pleasantly surprised that friends, using their own taste and their sense of what the couple might appreciate, are also sending presents. This may never have been strictly true, but it was a pleasant illusion for the guests to have. Miss Manners cannot fathom why those who are disabused of this are still motivated to demonstrate affection.

Sponsorship

DEAR MISS MANNERS—Will you please tell us where the custom originated of sponsors for weddings and debuts? Our neighbor is going around asking the neighbors for money for an expensive wedding. We think it is awful for people to impose on other people for money for their sons' or daughters' weddings. If you can't afford an expensive wedding, settle for what you can afford. We paid for our daughter's wedding, down to the last flower or mixed drink. We all try to do the best for our kids, but why should we pay for others?

GENTLE READER—The origin of this practice—Miss Manners refuses to dignify it by calling it a custom—is the strange idea that marriage is a justification for committing extortion. Miss Manners trusts that you will refuse to submit to this, without yourself being rude. You need merely decline the offer to be a "sponsor," and add that you send the couple your best wishes.

Collecting Cash

DEAR MISS MANNERS—HELP!! My daughter is getting married soon—a formal wedding—and she has just decided to carry a "Money Bag" during the reception!! She hopes to make enough money for a down payment on a house!!!

I'm appalled! Is this telling her friends, our friends, his friends that their gift is not enough, or is this something common in the '90s?? In my opinion, greed has overcome the young people and they don't celebrate the solemn occasion—they want to see how much money they can "make"!! If it is proper, maybe her father and I should carry one—a big one!!

GENTLE READER—Do you think you have put in enough exclamation points to express proper horror? Miss Manners finds an excess of them still perilously lodged in her own throat. She had better dispose of them discreetly, because you have actually given her two questions to answer:

1. Is it common in the '90s for bridal couples to go crazed with greed? Yes, although Miss Manners congratulates this couple on taking the impulse to new depths.
2. Is it proper? Don't make Miss Manners laugh while she has something in her throat.

You might inquire of your daughter whether she is under the impression that your friends and hers will be so emotionally overcome by the event of her marriage that they will be moved to help her buy a house. And furthermore, whether they will be too shy to accomplish such a wish unless she does them the favor of offering them an opportunity.

Otherwise, her scheme consists of simple social blackmail. She is counting on the guests forking over under the threat of embarrassment. This is not exactly what we call hospitality.

Miss Manners is unfortunately not confident that if the real nature of what your daughter and her fiancé are doing is drawn to their attention, they will back down. Why should people hesitate to induce a profitable false embarrassment in their friends when they have shown themselves willing to give their own parents cause for the intense, genuine embarrassment of blackmailing their friends? Miss Manners urges you to refuse to be a party to this. People who treat their wedding guests this way do not deserve to have any.

A Reply

DEAR MISS MANNERS—Miss Manners (I am loath to call you that) needs to do more research into other cultures and customs before condemning the young lady who wanted to carry a money satchel at her wedding. Both you and her mother were horrified, but just because you have your nose in the air, the young lady hardly invented it.

In the middle European communities (this includes many Polish, Russian, Italian, French and, I just learned, Vietnamese peoples) gifts are reserved for the wedding showers. When you attend a formal wedding with a sit-down dinner, at a banquet hall, the proper "gift" is an envelope with cash or check, which is left with the bride, who places it in the money bag.

If Miss Manners thinks her uppity manners prevail everywhere, she has another think coming. Those of us who are happy to celebrate our own customs await your apology, and a hope that the overbearing mother of this with-it new bride sees this before she ruins her daughter's wedding day.

Today, a banquet hall reception can run $75 to $100 or more per person. Many couples, whose parents aren't able to underwrite this tremendous bill, pay for the hall out of these monetary proceeds. My wife and I did this ourselves.

GENTLE READER—Miss Manners is not immune to the lure of tradition, and would not interfere when customs are practiced among those who developed them. Please forgive her, but in this case she does not quite understand the argument about being emotionally attached to a heritage of which the young lady's parents have never heard.

She also cautions those whom you characterize as "with it," against pleading tradition too strongly. Miss Manners has heard of a great many wedding traditions from these and other cultures, most of which have to do with verifying the virginity of the bride.

As life progresses, people weed out inherited practices they find offensive and dig up ones they find useful, such as you and this bride have done. By requiring guests to contribute toward putting on a wedding that the principals cannot afford, you are jettisoning the tradition of hospitality in favor of one called Living Above Your Means.

Settling Up

DEAR MISS MANNERS—I know there's no remedy for my problem. My husband and I had a beautiful, simple wedding (fifty-five guests) a year ago, at our house, which we planned and paid for ourselves. We're in our early thirties, were already living together, and both have full-time jobs. Needless to say, the wedding was a lot of work and expense, but at the time, we were happy we did it. The only thing marring a wonderful memory is that at least twelve of our closest friends who attended never gave us a wedding gift.

I realize it is verging on pettiness, but I wonder how many other couples experience this. Is this common, or do we just have an unusually large number of inconsiderate friends? I know I should never mention it to them, but my husband and I both find that we feel resentful toward these people. I am sure they probably figured they had a year after the wedding to get a gift and then just forgot, but I can't help it. I now look at these people and think they're selfish. I find I don't call them much.

One of these friends is getting married soon and I find myself evilly thinking, "This is our chance to not give them anything." Is this completely out of line? How do my husband and I get rid of this resentment that is now marring our friendships? I now wish we'd eloped.

GENTLE READER—Miss Manners doesn't know how many couples experience bitter regret at having had a simple and beautiful wedding because it did not achieve the goal of collecting tribute from every single person present. Nowadays, probably lots. What's the point in getting married without a 100 percent return in donations? As you may imagine, Miss Manners does not much care for this line of reasoning, which she agrees you have accurately character-ized as evil.

The remedy is to enjoy what ought to be your own hap-piness. However, after your year of improper brooding over deprivation, the situation has changed. You now find your-self in the position of being invited to be wedding guests, and therefore the question of whether to give presents or not is one that you may legitimately consider.

The custom of giving presents to help establish a new household has indeed been eroded, both because many bridal couples, such as yourselves, already have fully stocked households and because the potential recipients have become so frank about their expectations as to take the pleasure out of giving. Miss Manners would like to see the custom survive as a symbolic expression of good will on such an important occasion as marriage—but only if it can be maintained as a voluntary gesture, prompted by affection.

Should you no longer feel affection for your own wed-ding guests, you have no business attending their weddings. Should you still care for them, it seems to Miss Manners that you would want to participate in their happiness, not seize on an opportunity to slight them in revenge.

The Charity Wedding

DEAR MISS MANNERS—Since my fiancé and I are in our late thirties and have maintained households for many years, we do not need many of the things that people often give as wedding gifts. We are both active in volunteer activi-ties and we thought we would ask our friends and relatives to make a donation in our name to our favorite charity, in lieu of a wedding gift.

As we made this known, we found that several friends said they intend to give us a gift anyway. Do you have any suggestion as to how we can tactfully discourage these people? How should we handle the people who bring gifts to the reception anyway? We do not wish to embarrass them, but we also don't want people who followed our wishes to see a number of gifts and wonder if they, too, should have given a gift rather than a donation.

GENTLE READER—Miss Manners has a wonderful suggestion for you: Take all that time and effort you are putting into improperly denying others their privilege to decide what, if anything, they want to give you, and donate it to your favorite charity. As for people who do give you presents, your job is to thank them. The items are then yours, to use as you wish, which could include donating them to charity.

4

TERRIBLE IDEA III

The Wedding as Show Business

Miss Manners may be the only person who remembers when people got married by putting on the best clothes they already had, and going with a few similarly attired friends and relatives to their regular place of worship, where they followed a solemn and traditional ritual set by their religion.

Queen Victoria herself started the practice of costuming the bride in white (although we do not hold the dear lady responsible for the vulgar notion that this advertised that the body inside was untouched). From then on, it was all downhill, from solemnity and tradition to the flash and gimmicks of show business. There have always been similarities, theater having originated by copying the pageantry of religion, but now the direction has been reversed and the process accelerated.

Since the Academy Awards ceremony has been televised, it has been the quintessential modern ritual, setting the pattern for all others. The ingredients are: Outrageous clothing mixing all degrees of formality and informality, a pathway cleared for grand entrances, on-the-spot opinions solicited by bystanders, a patter of jokes and teasing from one or more masters of ceremonies, introductions of par-

A Silly Chorus Line

This is the unfortunate result when a bride cares more about having matching bridesmaids and costuming them to express her personal taste, such as it is, than that her bridesmaids be her dear friends, however dumpy, and suitably dressed.

The Ceremony

This is the basic plan for standing at the altar, with bridesmaids and ushers fetchingly grouped in the background. However, it is charming as well as proper to gather the couple's other parents and such children as might have arrived in the marriage by proper or improper means.

ticipants summarizing their biographies, time out and other inconveniences to accommodate the requirements of filming, choreographed chorus lines, rehearsed outpourings of gratitude and sentiment, standing ovations, sly references to the love lives of those present, presentations of trophies, acknowledgment of sponsors, and at least one impassioned plea on behalf of someone's favorite cause.

This has produced significant innovations in the wedding ritual:

Everyone is costumed, but none of it matches. The wedding party may be in formal clothes, but not even of the same degree of formality—for example, the bridegroom in white tie (or more likely, an "original" variation thereof) while the groomsmen are in black tie; and the guests dressed at an even less formal level, from business suits to jeans, on the grounds that they are audience, not performers.

Direction, jokes, and background anecdotes are offered at the reception by a professional master of ceremonies, while during the ceremony, the officiant tries valiantly to be equally entertaining and revealing.

The stars, seeing this as their moment in the spotlight, subordinate the form to showcase themselves by "personalizing" it with references to their love life and their philosophical beliefs. Being such, they are of course given the leeway of high temperament and indulged in whatever whims and selfishness they may care to exercise.

Family members and friends are cast into set roles, regardless of whom this includes or excludes: a man to give the bride away, even if there is no father—the mother not being considered for the part—and attendants chosen for the right look and number, rather than solely for being close friends.

The bride's mother's entrance has become a staged event, as a prelude to the bride's entrance, which pulls people to their feet. Applause and ovations are common, especially for the first marital kiss (which also draws laughter, as if it were a love scene viewed by an audience of early adolescents) and the pronouncement of the marriage (or maybe that round of clapping is because the show is ending).

Presents are regarded as admission tickets, and there is a lot of anger at those who try to get in without them. These are brought to the event and handed over, regardless of the logistical difficulties this creates, because paying admission has become so important a part of the occasion.

Finally, capturing the event on film for another audience is treated as superseding any need to accommodate those actually present. Guests may be shoved aside or made to endure long blank waits, or cast without warning as extras, if the film script calls for candid reaction interviews.

Miss Manners is only too aware of the unpopularity of the position she is taking. Nobody loves a critic. Why shouldn't a wedding be entertainment and draw on the experience of professionals in the business?

Her first reason is that this is often bad theater, and she is not the only critic. Not every amateur, no matter how in love, can produce a good original script. It is one thing to have friends murmuring "I thought the church needed more flowers," and quite another to hand them your courtship and philosophy to critique.

The second is that a wedding should be a joyous but serious occasion, rather than lighthearted entertainment. It's marriage itself, not the ceremony, that is supposed to be a scream.

The Program

DEAR MISS MANNERS—It has come to my attention that I must have a program at my wedding, because "everyone" has a program at their weddings. Quite frankly, I cannot recall one at the weddings I have attended, but most likely I would not have kept it. The examples I have been given not only have the wedding ceremony, but a "list of characters" from the bride and groom down to the hostesses (not necessarily the parents, but rather a wedding consultant or caterer) and "acknowledgments," listing the florist, travel agent, facility, etc. I've been told that they help guests identify who's in the wedding and they can refer back to them should they forget a name, but the idea of having a program is not sitting quite well with me.

GENTLE READER—Where else would you put the plot summary? And the synopsis of what happened to lead up to this event? And the preview of what may happen next? How else could you credit the sponsors? Introduce the actors ("Sherrie is a newlywed herself and a new mother," "Mike especially enjoys water sports")? The only excuse for a program is to give the order of the service, which is not necessary at a wedding. Here we have yet another show business touch, treating the wedding ceremony as entertainment, and supplying the accessories associated with it. Miss Manners congratulates you on resisting.

The Cast

DEAR MISS MANNERS—My son by a previous marriage is to marry soon. His mother died while he was a minor, and two older sisters became surrogate mothers in her stead. He wishes to acknowledge this at the reception by announcing them together with myself as a part of that ceremony. My present wife feels slighted by this, and feels emphatically that a provision should be made to present her as my wife, as well. She refuses to attend otherwise.

GENTLE READER—Announcing? Presenting? Does Miss Manners understand you to ask who gets the public credit for being the bridegroom's surrogate mother? See the trouble people get into by treating their weddings as show business award ceremonies? A wedding is a family gathering, not a contest. There is no need to announce, "And in the role of mother . . ." Why shouldn't the four of you occupy the front pew, sit at a family table at the reception, and receive his toasts of thanks?

The Extras

DEAR MISS MANNERS—My fiancé and I are trying to find a mature and nice way of requesting on our invitation that there be no crying children at the wedding, due to the professional videotaping. What is the best way of telling guests without offending them?

GENTLE READER—What makes you think that your younger guests are more likely than the older ones to be overcome with sentiment on the occasion of your marriage, and to weep through the service? Anyway, wouldn't this add a tender note to your professional videotape, bound to touch the hearts of audiences everywhere when the tape is released in neighborhood theaters?

Or is it, Miss Manners finally understands, that you assume that all children cry, simply as recreation, especially when asked to sit still for an hour? In that case, don't invite any children to your wedding. Should their parents inquire whether this was an inadvertent omission, you must say, with a tone of regret so as not to seem a monster, "Oh, I'm so sorry, but we're not having any children there. I know yours would behave perfectly, but others might find it tedious." This is more acceptable than "I'm not using children in my show." (See The Guest List, page 70.)

The Bridegroom's Clothes

A polite bridegroom takes care not to be more eye-catching than the bride. He may wear white tie(*above, center*) or black tie(*right*) if the wedding takes place after six, morning clothes(*left*) for a formal daytime wedding, or a business suit(*bottom*) for an informal wedding at any time. He does not dress differently from the other gentlemen in the bridal party, and the wedding guests are supposed to dress formally if he does, as surprised and indignant as they may be to hear this.

The Costumes

DEAR MISS MANNERS—Within hours of their engagement, my nephew's betrothed joined the congregation of a very picturesque church to provide a suitable venue for her special event. The wedding is almost upon us, and the bride has announced that hats are NOT to be worn.

Other than the fact that my two young daughters and I have already purchased lovely bonnets to complement the chosen setting, how can we enter a house of worship for an afternoon wedding, bareheaded? Is it no longer customary to cover one's head in a church? Would a lace handkerchief or designer tissue do?

GENTLE READER—If your prospective niece has changed her church merely in order to acquire the background scenery she wants, nothing is going to persuade her that she cannot costume the extras. That, Miss Manners regrets to say, is what she seems to think her wedding guests are.

As you have noticed, the bride's idea about hats is wrong, in addition to being impertinent. It is proper, although no longer mandatory, for ladies to wear hats both for any church service and for any afternoon wedding. So perhaps you are entitled to wear two hats.

It would be even worse to appear with patterned nose-wipes on your head, if Miss Manners understands you correctly, or with lace handkerchiefs (although many a lady made do with such when the Catholic Church barred bareheaded ladies from the door).

Nor do you want to start a family feud with a new relative who is unpleasant enough without provocation. Miss Manners would therefore suggest either sending back the message about your already purchased hats through your nephew (who supposedly knows how to deal

Mr. and Mrs. Samuel McGee

request the pleasure of your company

at a reception

in the honor of

Ms. Heather Brittany Right-Megabyte and Mr. Daniel McGee

on Saturday, the fifteenth of July

at eight o'clock

The Marge Club

Lake Lebarge, Alaska

Please reply
1 Marge Drive
Lake Lebarge, Alaska   78877

The solution to the bridegroom's parents' grumbling that not enough of their friends were able to attend the wedding is the delayed reception to honor the newly married couple, rather than a road show repeat of the wedding itself.

with this person), or simply wearing flowers or ribbons in your hair.

Facing the Audience

DEAR MISS MANNERS—My daughter faced the audience during her wedding vows, as did the rest of the wedding party. It was a treat to see the ceremony, facing the expressions, and the beautiful bridesmaids and the men. I realize that some ceremonies must be conducted with certain rites that must have the wedding party's backs to the viewers. However, some ministers or pastors would not object to having their backs to the audience. Perhaps you could suggest this?

GENTLE READER—The "audience"? Is that what you think the people are who gather in a house of worship to witness a sacred ritual? Miss Manners has been increasingly aware that, weddings now being regarded as a popular amateur branch of show business, not only spirituality but also ties and duties to family and friends have become secondary to the production values. Your suggestion, however, is original enough to manage to shock her. As you are dabbling in theater, she suggests that you analyze the symbolism you plan to convey: In facing their audience, to Whom would these star-for-a-day performers be turning their backs?

Playing to an Empty House

DEAR MISS MANNERS—This is a worst-case scenario:

A wedding is planned and the bridesmaids, having bought their expensive dresses, are thrilled at being asked to participate in such a socially prestigious event. But then the invitations arrive and the wedding is to be held in the bride's home town, 200 miles away. The groom's relatives live in the opposite direction. Arrangements have been made to accommodate out-of-town guests (and the wedding party) in a nearby city; the rates are reasonable as weekend rates go, but the guests pay their own way. Times being hard and distance and expense outweighing fond sentiment, the regrets are 100 percent.

Then what happens? Can the bridesmaids and ushers bow out? The mother of the groom certainly would, if given half a chance, and she is not at all certain her dress will arrive in time. Do the bride's parents send out cancellation notices and let the couple marry in their own city and among their close friends?

At least the hosts will be spared the problem of what to do about the wedding presents people bring along to the reception, and the problem of the uninvited guests people bring along because there won't be anyone they know to talk to—supposing one could talk in the ear-shattering din of loud dance music. Wouldn't it be a welcome end to all the show-biz extravaganza? And might not a return to the small, intimate, and meaningful ceremony result in lower divorce statistics?

GENTLE READER—Miss Manners is no fonder of the show business mentality toward weddings than you are, but she finds herself unable to gloat at the picture of people who discover that no one cares enough about them to attend their wedding. The idea that even their intimates are tempted to bail out now is pathetic.

However pretentious the bridal couple may be, surely it is their invited guests who have a distasteful attitude. As you point out, convenience and price have outweighed sentiment. Had they cared, they might have hopped a bus and inquired about staying with the couple's local friends and relatives. One does not absolutely require an "audience," as it were, for a wedding of any style. If they were planning this wedding to dazzle others, yes, it should be canceled if those others won't be there. If they were doing it for their own satisfaction, Miss Manners does not see why they should not go ahead with it.

5

THE ENGAGEMENT

Proposing

Which is the more up-to-the-minute and fashionable way for a modern couple to reach a definitive agreement that they will be married?

Scenario One:

This takes place in the household that the couple already share, at a time neither of them has scheduled. Either person can initiate the conversation, as long as this is done in an acrimonious tone. The subject is provoked by a piece of information from the outside—a wedding invitation from another couple, an inquiry from a parent, a photograph of a baby in a magazine, a newspaper feature declaring a trend in the way people live. If the idea of marriage is not rejected out of hand, the next session is a businesslike negotiation. Terms are debated: Whose money would be whose? How would future work, such as child rearing, be divided? What contingencies would there be in case the marriage failed? If that is concluded successfully, discussions of wedding plans begin with the mention of an engagement ring. Will there be one? How will it be chosen? How will it be financed—by the gentleman alone, or should the lady contribute equally? Can she contribute more in order to upgrade what he might be able to afford, on the grounds that it is she who will be wearing it?

Scenario Two:

The gentleman secretly plans a special occasion and lures the lady to conform with his plans without her guessing the purpose. If she does, she is obliged to preserve the illusion by pretending to be bewildered. The setting he has chosen has sentimental associations, or luxurious or romantic characteristics, or as many and much of these as his imagination and resources allow. He is on his most courtly and attentive behavior, but he draws things out for the maximum suspense. At the great moment, he brings out an engagement ring that he has chosen and bought by himself. Perhaps he hides it somewhere clever for her to find (food seems to be the hiding place of choice), or perhaps he just produces it dramatically as he pronounces the age-old formula, "Will you marry me?" She appears to be overcome with confusion and emotion. After a suitable period of blushing and protesting her amazement, she agrees to allow him to slip the ring on her finger. Then one or the other must bring up the next business at hand, which is when and how he will ask her parents' permission to marry her.

Which do you think is today's cutting edge form of marriage proposal?

Call her old-fashioned, but Miss Manners had thought it was Scenario One. Even her cloistered ears have heard that young people do not nowadays agree to marry after a mere kiss on the parental front porch and that they have perhaps not preserved their innocence about financial matters and other practical considerations.

Yet she seems to have been mistaken. Scenario Two is becoming more and more the prevailing tradition. True, those who practice it are not generally in their first youth or first stages of courtship. It has even been suggested to her that it is for that very reason that they want the trappings of romance and the ceremonies of the past.

Miss Manners is aware that the gentleman may have to remind himself not to conclude the meal by saying, "Don't think we're going to split this down the middle—you had dessert and I didn't." She knows that the following week, the lady who needed her parents' permission to be married may be indignant that they think they have anything to say about the wedding arrangements. But for the moment, Miss Manners would just like to bask in the charm of the revived ritual. She has not a word of advice to add—except perhaps that they both pay sufficient attention to avoid ending up in the Emergency Room because the lady has swallowed the ring.

Her Proposal

DEAR MISS MANNERS—During courtship, there is typically a period of "testing the waters" for marriage. In this day and age, I do not believe that a lady must necessarily wait for her suitor to propose, assuming that if he hasn't asked her, he is not ready to marry her. I think it would be romantic for a gentleman to receive an (albeit unconventional) proposal from the woman he loves.

What is the correct etiquette for proposing to a man? Does the lady still wear an engagement ring? If so, should it be bought in advance or after, by him, her, or both together? Should she offer her fiancé a ring or some other token of her commitment? Finally, does this alter in any way the traditional divisions of responsibility and costs of the wedding?

GENTLE READER—Miss Manners wishes people would understand that there is a difference between one gender's claiming a privilege that was once associated with the other and completely switching genders. Proposing to the gentleman does not make her—if he accepts—the bridegroom. Nor would he wear the bridal veil at the wedding.

There is nothing wrong with a lady's proposing marriage to a gentleman; it is not even all that unconventional. That's what old-fashioned feminine probings to find out the seriousness of a suitor's intentions were all about.

As for the wording, a marriage proposal should concentrate on one person's passionate desire to be united to the other. Miss Manners might have considered that obvious but for all the people who believe that "It's about time" or "I'm not getting any younger" are just as effective. They aren't. Tell him that you can't wait to begin your lives together.

The part about the ring is best left out. Gentlemen do not wear engagement rings (Miss Manners is not listening to the cry of tradespeople who want to supply such items) and a lady's giving herself an engagement ring tends to suggest that the gentleman's role in the relationship will be a negligible one.

Having accepted a marriage proposal does not in any way prevent a gentleman from giving his fiancée an engagement ring if he feels so inclined. From the time he accepts, they become an engaged couple and proceed in their plans as they would otherwise have done.

Parental Permission

DEAR MISS MANNERS—My son is planning to become engaged to a wonderful girl who has had a strict upbringing and has only recently broken away from a matriarch-mother. His fiancée is aware of this and has been friendly and sociable.

My son asked if it would help matters if he would first mention the engagement to the mother (the girl's father has died) to let her feel she is part of their plans. Or is that never done with engagements—that being a private happy time for the two involved. Is it still proper and considerate for my son to ask the mother for "her daughter's hand" and "blessing for the marriage"? He wants to do the right thing in order to continue gaining the mother's approval.

GENTLE READER—Your son has charming instincts and Miss Manners has only small adjustments to suggest to him. Even in stricter times, a gentleman interested in a romantic match—as opposed to making a business deal with a lady's family and depending on them to extract her compliance—always made sure of the lady before approaching her family.

In this case, your hint about mother-daughter friction makes it seem especially wise first to make sure of her feelings about his idea, as well as her feelings about him.

The proper order is therefore:

1. Ask young lady for her hand in marriage.
2. Ask young lady for permission to ask her mother for her hand in marriage.
3. Ask mother.

The Prenuptial Contract

"Daddy's being horrid," the bride-to-be would say in simpler times. "He wants to know all about the money—as if I cared about money! All I care about is you. His stupid solicitors are even asking about dowager rights. That's disgusting. Why, if anything happened to you—or if I thought you didn't love me any more—I wouldn't need any money, because I'd just kill myself."

Her fiancé would take her hand in his, glancing around to make sure no one was looking. "My parents are just as bad," he would confide. "Money, property—my mother wanted to know what would happen to the family pearls if I predeceased you and you married again. You wouldn't marry again, would you? Of course not. Me neither. I'm beginning to think they can't ever have been in love themselves. No one who understood how I feel about you could even think of material things."

Thus the happy couple could snuggle up against each other in perfect understanding and love, while her family lawyers and his family lawyers hammered out an agreement that represented each of their interests should the unthinkable occur.

Miss Manners does not recount this tale to suggest that all does not always turn out as the affianced imagine, nor even to warn that they should prepare themselves in case it doesn't. She believes in true love. She is merely pointing out that concerns about the eventual disposition of money and property when a marriage begins is not a new phenomenon. The Victorians knew how to handle it a lot better than modern couples who are looking out for their own interests.

The modern approach is that the bridegroom (or whichever of the couple is richer) shoves a document into the bride's face the day, or perhaps only hours, before the wedding, and says, "Here, you have to sign this." At any reluctance, he threatens to call off the marriage. By this time, she would be only too glad to be rid of him, but she feels a sense of responsibility to the caterer. So she signs.

It is true that in the antique version, it was entirely possible that the gentleman would eventually run off with the governess and that the lady not only did not kill herself, but, as he was able to show, had long since been consoling herself with the curate.

However, in the modern version, disillusion and bitterness have set in *before* the wedding has taken place. The thought of coercion may appear during the ceremony itself, whereas in the olden days, the financial arrangement had been kept entirely separate from the courtship. The agreement by which she had to give back the pearls and he was unable to touch her family property had been cheerfully made between two parties, either parents or their representatives, whose business sense was unclouded by emotions.

Miss Manners suggests that anyone interested in a prenuptial agreement about finances return to the ancestral wisdom. Perhaps there are no parents around willing to involve themselves in the transaction, but one may still blame others for being unromantic, even if one has hired them for the purpose.

Miss Manners recommends a version of the following dialogue:

"Oh, darling, I wish we were married already. There's so much to do, and I just want to be alone with you."

"Ummmmm. Me, too."

"Did you call about the cake?"

"I thought you were going to do that."

"That's right—I will. I'm sorry. Oh, and then there's another thing. My lawyer has done some property agreement—what happens if I die, or whatever."

"Don't even think such a thing. I couldn't live without you. What's in it? Where is it?"

"Darling, I don't even know. I find the whole thing degrading. I'm just going to have my lawyer send it over to your lawyer. Now come here."

The Engagement Announcement and Presents

DEAR MISS MANNERS—I received a formal, engraved engagement announcement; the couple does not plan to be married any time soon. Is a gift required, or even appropriate?

GENTLE READER—Traditionally, there is no such thing as a private, formal engagement announcement, as opposed to general announcements in newspapers. People are supposed to let their friends know the happy news by telephone, letter, or other informal means.

Miss Manners does not want to suggest that your friends had any ulterior motive for inventing a new form. Perhaps they fell under the influence of a stationer who had an ulterior motive. Perhaps they have more friends than they can possibly keep in touch with using the normal methods, although that does seem to make nonsense out of the definition of friendship. In any case, the response is the same as if they had written that friendly note. Write back, congratulating them and wishing them happiness.

No presents are necessary at this time. People who care enough about the principals to attend a wedding are supposed to express this symbolically by means of a wedding present, but it takes a great deal more spontaneous affection to want to give an engagement present. The only traditional (but also not obligatory) one is the ring that the prospective bridegroom gives the prospective bride.

The Engagement Ring

THE PRESENTATION

DEAR MISS MANNERS—I have been engaged for nearly nine months, but my fiancé and I have recently bought my engagement ring together. My mother is upset with us, because she says that the ring is supposed to be given to me at the engagement party and that I am not supposed to see it until then. Is there any truth to this saying?

GENTLE READER—No, Miss Manners is afraid not. She doesn't want to encourage you to engage in etiquette battles with your mother—the two of you have a wedding yet to get through—but she knows of no such custom.

Presentation of an engagement ring is necessarily a private event. A party is to announce that the engagement already exists—not to allow people to witness its being made.

THE RING SIZE

DEAR MISS MANNERS—I am a divorced male whose fiancée is also divorced and marrying for the second time. What is the currently accepted protocol for engagement rings in second marriages? Also, must my fiancée's ring necessarily be larger than the one given by her ex-husband to his current fiancée?

GENTLE READER—The correct formula is to multiply the size of the lady's first engagement ring by the size of the one you gave your first wife and add to it the size of the ring her former husband gave his fiancée. With any luck, you will soon reach a stalemate, with the gentlemen no longer able to afford to raise the stakes and the ladies no longer able to lift their hands, and Miss Manners will be able to turn her attention to sensible questions.

6

THE SHOWER

In proper American etiquette, a bridal shower is a lighthearted event among intimate friends, not something required to call attention to a wedding in the way that a rain shower calls attention to the need to fetch an umbrella. Bridal showers are supposed to be thought up and given by the hostesses, never by the guest of honor or her relatives. The bride should act pleased and surprised if one is spontaneously suggested to her by her friends. No one should be invited to more than one such event for the occasion. Presents should be mere tokens.

However, we live in an age of entitlement. In her darker moments, Miss Manners wonders if the shower hasn't become more important than the wedding itself. The shower has been perceived as one more opportunity to turn a milestone to material advantage and all these rules are being violated right and left. This should neither exonerate those who practice intimidation, nor discourage guests from abiding by the rules of etiquette always available to them: They may decline the invitation, sending nothing more than their good wishes. Some couples used to think that in itself was quite valuable.

The Enemies List

DEAR MISS MANNERS—Scenario One: Several family members are not speaking. One is getting married and indicates she will probably send an invitation to everyone in the family, regardless of their differences. Should the individuals giving a surprise bridal shower invite these estranged family members to the shower, prior to the bride reconciling with her family?

Scenario Two: The bride indicates she is not inviting the members of the family from whom she is estranged. Should they be invited to a shower given for the bride?

GENTLE READER—At first glance, these seemed like two terrible ideas. Showers are occasions on which people overflowing with love gather around their dear friend and these guests are unlikely candidates.

This certainly rules out Scenario Two. To expect people to fuss over a bride who does not speak to them is not a socially sound idea.

Scenario One might have its advantages, however. Gathering former enemies at a wedding is not without danger and to hold a less formal event as a trial run is not a bad idea.

Shower By Mail

DEAR MISS MANNERS—I have been asked to be maid of honor for a good friend who lives quite a distance away. Her fiancé lives in another part of the country and nearly all the invited guests reside all over the country and in Europe. How am I to throw a shower for the bride? Is it proper to have a "shower by mail" where people send gifts on a certain day?

GENTLE READER—A shower is a party, Miss Manners feels it necessary to remind you. What you are describing is a mail solicitation, which is not regulated by etiquette but by the Post Office.

A "Stag and Doe"

DEAR MISS MANNERS—One of my coworkers approached me with the information that she and her fiancé were having a "Stag and Doe" prior to their marriage and inquired as to whether I would like to purchase a ticket for a certain sum to attend.

Shouldn't someone other than the bride-to-be be handling the sale of these tickets? I've always freely contributed to gifts purchased as a group by coworkers in our large office, but I admit that I was startled and embarrassed by this direct request.

GENTLE READER—What do you think might be more genteel? Involving Ticketron?

The fact is that the concept of a wedding as a frankly acknowledged fund-raising event is so vulgar as to make the details seem hardly worth refining. We have rapidly gone from a bridal couple's appreciating the generosity of their friends and relatives to their expecting it, to their directing it, to their demanding it—and not only of their personal ties, but of their professional ones, as well.

What puzzles Miss Manners is why anyone gives in to this unattractive pressure. An event that requires tickets is paid amusement, not social life. Whatever this person is charging, Miss Manners guesses that you could buy more amusement at the movies.

Although come to think of it, she might blow a small admission price to find the answer to the Stag and Doe Riddle: If a stag event is one for males only, as opposed to the normal social event that includes both males and females; and a doe event is one for females only, as opposed to the normal social event that includes both males and females—what in heaven's name is a stag and doe event? Open hunting season on predatory creatures?

Combining Baby and Bridal Showers

DEAR MISS MANNERS—Please help fast! Time is running out. A friend is having a baby soon, and she and the baby's father have agreed to wait until a month after the baby is born to get married. Can we combine a baby and bridal shower, or is it unethical to ask people to bring two gifts? We really don't have the time for two separate showers.

GENTLE READER—How fast? Miss Manners is out of breath. It's not just from rushing (if her usual stately pace can be speeded up at all). The breath was knocked out of her by that incidental remark about the couple's wanting to wait until after the birth to be married. Has the purpose of marriage so changed that it is more important how the bride looks at the wedding than that the baby be born within the marriage? Hand Miss Manners her smelling salts and don't bother reminding her that this aspect is none of her business.

Yes, holding two showers for the same person would strain the patience even of friends. But so would expecting them to bring separate presents to one shower. As your friend has combined being a bride and being a mother, there is no reason that your shower honoring her should not do so as well, allowing people to choose items appropriate to either aspect of her new life.

Games and Prizes

DEAR MISS MANNERS—A friend of mine is giving a bridal shower at which games are to be played. There will be prizes for the winners. But it seems that where my friend came from, it is the practice not for the winners to keep their prizes, but to be asked to give them all to the bride-to-be. Since every guest brings a gift for the bride, it seems that guests ought to be able to take home whatever little game gifts they have won. Maybe I'm wrong but it seems a waste of time to even play.

GENTLE READER—Where your friend comes from, it is no doubt the custom for birthday children to grab prizes back from their little guests. Miss Manners would not have thought that these people would grow up to have bridal showers. It is strange enough to imagine how they might find guests still willing to be treated so selfishly, let alone people to marry. Whatever the origin of this custom, it must be stopped immediately. Miss Manners can hardly think of a worse preparation for marriage than to allow the bride to believe that she should always win, regardless of whether or not this is fair.

7

THE
GUEST LIST

For years, Miss Manners let pass without comment (or much interest) the first rule of planning a wedding that she knew bridal couples are commonly told. Figure out the size you want your wedding to be, they are cautioned. This is determined not only by your taste, but by your budget. When you know what you want the style of the wedding to be and what you can afford to spend to make it so, you will realize how many guests you can invite. That number should then be divided evenly between the bride's family and the bridegroom's.

Not exactly fighting words, Miss Manners had supposed. Wedding size is not a decision based on etiquette, she told herself to assuage her conscience about her wandering attention. A proper wedding can consist of only the principals, or can include an entire nation lining the streets, simultaneously cheering and memorizing the design of the wedding dress for cheaper reproduction.

Certainly no one should be financially strained for the sake of a wedding. Contrary to unpleasant belief, etiquette has never tried to dictate who should spend what on a wedding. The only stake that etiquette has in the wedding size is making sure that people who legitimately expect to be invited—there are a lot of illegitimate expectations floating around society these days, which their possessors are not shy of mentioning—are not hurt.

Alert readers will have noticed the lapse of logic that so long escaped Miss Manners. Suppose the size you decide upon, either because you prefer it or because that is all you can afford, or both, is smaller than the number of people who will be hurt if not invited?

Of course Miss Manners said you couldn't hurt them, not that you had to invite them. To avoid doing both, you must limit the list by categories unrelated to individual likes or dislikes. "There are so many close friends we would love to have, but we're having just a private ceremony with members of the immediate family," is a polite explanation that ought to satisfy any reasonable friend. So is "We're not having any children," or "We've had to define 'family' only as far as first cousins, not second cousins."

What of the common variation of this—"We'd love to invite everybody, but we can only afford to have x people?" It has belatedly occurred to Miss Manners that there is something inherently rude in allowing style and cost to prevail over emotional bonds. When something has to be cut, it should be the menu and frills, not the guests. Let us say, for example, that you have a large family or a huge circle of friends who truly care about you and with whom you would like to share your wedding, but feeding them all dinner is prohibitive. The solution is to feed them all wedding cake and punch, rather than to feed everything to only a few of them. All that is required is not to set the wedding near a mealtime.

While the idea of dividing the list between the two families—or four sets of parents, as can easily happen nowadays—is a fair one, polite people will be flexible enough to count guests by relationship, rather than number. If he has six uncles and she has none, it would be thoughtful to fit the list to his family, without the bride's demanding to throw in six extra acquaintances to make things even.

Miss Manners would like to hear of the families planning together by asking first, "Whom would you like to have?" and only afterward, "Well, let's see. What can we afford to feed them?" It would be an excellent introduction, Miss Manners believes, to the special definition of fairness and generosity essential to a successful marriage.

Inviting Children

DEAR MISS MANNERS—I've been told that children should not attend a formal wedding reception, but I've been to several where children were present. I have many young cousins and a niece and nephew and am unsure how to handle this situation when I get married next June.

GENTLE READER—There are two schools of thought about children attending weddings—one that holds that they are adorable and add to the spirit of the occasion, and the other that they are unruly and bound to be a nuisance.

Miss Manners holds to the former. It seems to her that weddings being the joining of two families, as well as of two individuals who happen to have a yen for each other, children are an appropriate part. Of course, she is assuming reasonably polite children, which may be rather a leap these days.

She does not therefore condemn those who take the other view. But children must then be excluded by age, the good with the bad. Pointing out who behaves like a piggy is just not good for family relations.

A-List and B-List

DEAR MISS MANNERS—My very close brother-in-law had a lovely wedding with a dream reception, but some feelings were hurt. My husband was his best man. My parents, I, and my two children were invited. We were told they were glad to have my two boys, that there would be lots of children there, and there were.

The wedding was at one o'clock with a reception, and then a catered dinner served at four o'clock. Those who were invited to the dinner received a special invitation. My parents' names were not on the list, so they left quietly, not to cause a big scene. My name was on the list, but my children's names were not. The other children were all seated. I felt I couldn't stay.

Now I'm the bad guy! Because I didn't make a big scene and holler, I have hurt the newlyweds' feelings.

GENTLE READER—There is some unfortunate and legitimate confusion in this situation, but tell your relatives that Miss Manners does not approve of hollering as a way of settling etiquette problems. The problem is that tradition allowed wedding guests to be separated into A and B lists—some invited to both the ceremony and the festivities afterward, and others to one of those events but not the other.

Miss Manners no longer permits this. All guests other than immediate family may be invited to the celebration only, after a private ceremony, or asked to attend a ceremony not followed by a celebration, but some guests cannot be told to arrive after, or go home before, other guests. Child guests—as opposed to a child of the bride or bridegroom—are an exception, but those of the same age must be treated alike.

Thus, you and your parents should have been included for all the events and your children should have, as well, if others of the same age were. Had all the children been excluded from part of the activities and a nearby play area with baby-sitter not provided, their parents should have been told in advance so that arrangements could be made for them.

Too Many Friends

DEAR MISS MANNERS—I imagine many women in their thirties are grappling with the same problem I am about wedding invitations. The older you are, the more friends you've accumulated over the years. In deciding whom to invite, I go back to circles of friends from graduate school and college—circles where I've kept in touch with perhaps half of each group, yet attended all of their weddings. I'm wondering where to draw the line. Do I send invitations to the people I'm still close with and only announcements to my fading friends (who will inevitably hear through the grapevine that I'm getting married)? Or invitations to everyone and just hope there's a natural attrition rate?

GENTLE READER—Miss Manners cannot claim that it is rude to invite only close friends to one's wedding and send announcements to those now more distant. That is the correct distinction to make. But she would like to persuade you to issue invitations all around, anyway.

There is a sequel to that "older you get" formula that applies to late middle age: The older you get, the more you value the friends of your youth. Your now-fading friends will, of course, remember that you attended their weddings, and will therefore feel slightly miffed not to be invited to yours. It is, indeed, likely that they would not rush to attend, but the omission of an invitation would stick in their minds and might act as a barrier when you reach the stage of wanting to renew your old ties.

Faraway Friends

DEAR MISS MANNERS—My husband's and my relatives and friends live so far away that it will be an expense for them to come out to our daughter's wedding, much as we would like to have them. Is it correct to include a note acknowledging that we will understand if they cannot attend? Are we to provide hotel rooms?

GENTLE READER—Please do not even think about sending such a note. Miss Manners knows you mean well, but she is virtually certain that your relatives and friends will interpret it as evidence that your invitation is insincere, and you are hoping that they won't accept so that you can invite people you'd rather have in their place.

A great many people with good intentions decide not to send wedding invitations to those whom they believe will not accept (typically because they find travel difficult, are presumed not to be able to afford it, or live far away). All they succeed in doing is making the non-invitees feel unwanted.

It is not the task of hosts to answer, as well as issue, invitations. That is up to the guests. If they must decline, they can easily do so without even having to cite reasons. Oddly enough, they believe they make their own decisions better than anyone else can do for them.

No, you don't have to provide hotel rooms for wedding guests. However, if you really want them there and are worried about their expenses, it would be a gracious way to help.

One Spouse Only

DEAR MISS MANNERS—A colleague of my husband handed him an unaddressed wedding invitation and said something unclear about inviting him "for professional reasons." He told her he would like to attend the wedding, at which point she made it clear that the invitation did not extend to his wife. My husband plans to attend the wedding, because he genuinely wishes her well. It is of no emotional consequence to me whether I attend and of course I won't, as per the bride's wishes.

But has the bride been rude by inviting one member of a couple but not the other? If it is a rudeness, against whom has it been committed—my husband, who was discomfited to explain the situation to me, or me, who was excluded but feel no pain thereby?

GENTLE READER—Against Miss Manners, who was neither discomfited nor interested in the wedding, but who must guard the world against crimes of etiquette.

To invite someone to one's wedding "for professional reasons" is an unspeakable idea, which was only emphasized by not inviting you both as a couple, which is the way married people are treated in social life. Whatever career advantage the bride hopes to gain by treating your husband in this insulting fashion, Miss Manners cannot imagine what advantage he hopes to obtain by accepting. Probably none—probably he was just kind (or sweetly naive) enough not to be outraged. If you don't have the heart to explain to him that the bride obviously did not want him to accept, Miss Manners doesn't either.

Colleagues

DEAR MISS MANNERS—Surely you do not cling to the quaint notion that all wedding guests are intimates of the bride or groom. That may have been true once, but today many invited guests have never met either of them.

Consider the situation my husband and I have encountered, not once but twice. The president of a small company has a son or daughter who is getting married, and he thinks it would be jolly if he invited the whole management team. We could hardly not accept, although I resented being forced to buy a gift for someone I did not know. We attended the weddings, even though one was a hundred miles away.

Like you, I do not condone rudeness. If I accept an invitation, I do my utmost to fulfill the obligation. However,

I can understand someone in the situations I described who finds something more enjoyable to do than get dressed up to watch two strangers get married, and then stand in line with a couple hundred others for the standard hotel fare of fried chicken, ham, and overcooked vegetables. So they figure if they are on record as having accepted and sent the required gift, they can safely spend the day as they wish.

GENTLE READER—Miss Manners assures you that the hosts would rather have their guests safely on record as having declined the invitation than prepare for the comfort of those who do not show up. Not that she is in great sympathy with people who invite their business associates to a private occasion in which these people can have no genuine interest. It is almost asking them to treat it as a business meeting—one attends if one can, but not if something more important comes up. Nevertheless, a civilized person would resist that temptation. Spoiling someone's wedding reception—as would happen if the entire management team failed to arrive to take their designated places—is not the way to teach one's boss a lesson.

Volunteer Guests

DEAR MISS MANNERS—How can I explain to coworkers I do not socialize with that they are not invited to my wedding? Several people have mistakenly assumed they are invited, although I have never given them any indication that they would be and my guest list is above and beyond what I had hoped for. I really do not want to hurt their feelings, but I am put on the spot when they make these comments.

GENTLE READER—Rude as it is for people to let on that they expect to be invited to a wedding—especially people who are not in your social circle—you are right to handle them delicately. It is a rough desire to wish you well that leads them into this awkward error.

Your reply must be that you are having a very small wedding, only for your family and immediate circle of close friends. Never mind that other coworkers will be invited— you are quite right to count people only by whether you see them socially and not by what jobs they hold.

A wedding is not a professional occasion. And a small wedding is not necessarily one to which very few people are invited. It is one to which the person you are addressing is not invited.

Explanations

DEAR MISS MANNERS—My daughter and her fiancé have chosen a very small place for their wedding reception. As a result, the guest list has been painfully cut and there will be hurt feelings on both sides of the family as well as among friends. Would it be impolite or presumptuous to send letters to those who will not be invited, in order to explain the circumstances? Or would it be best left unmentioned, letting them wonder why they weren't invited and not addressing the situation at all?

GENTLE READER—What is the letter going to say? "We had to choose between having the wedding in a charming little place without you, or in an ordinary place with you, and we decided the heck with your hurt feelings—the location was more important to us than your presence"?

Miss Manners is afraid that it is impossible to escape the realization that such was the reasoning that led to your decision. She would not attempt to explain this to the excluded guests, if she were you. Rather, you might throw a party for the bridal couple upon their return from their wedding trip and invite those people to what you can still call a wedding reception.

Compensatory Entertaining

DEAR MISS MANNERS—Due to finances and my choice of location, I have limited my upcoming wedding to 100 guests. This means that some of my future mother-in-law's friends will be excluded. She is therefore insistent on including them in the rehearsal dinner at her home the night before, to which she has invited my bridesmaids only verbally through me, and ignored the clergy entirely. She also will not permit me to send wedding announcements to any of her friends.

These are only four examples of her endless lack of cooperation with my plans. I feel that rules of etiquette exist to protect all parties in any such situation, and prevent present anger and future discord. Am I justified in seeing these as breaches which put my parents and me in a very awkward situation?

GENTLE READER—There is an unpleasant thought that is preventing Miss Manners from entering sympathetically into the denunciation of your mother-in-law, which you kindly pair with a declaration of belief in etiquette.

It is that your case for courtesy seems to be built on the idea that you may blithely omit this lady's friends from wedding plans that you identify as yours, rather than both families'. It seems to Miss Manners that the awkwardness you describe stems from the mother of the bridegroom trying to recover from this slight.

The number of guests invited to a wedding is properly determined by the number of people whom each family wants to have present. Miss Manners is not saying that an exaggerated list cannot be argued down, but that those who are truly close to the family should not be dismissed with the claim of saving money.

You could limit the wedding to family and throw related parties for friends. Had there been more sympathy shown all around, it could have been suggested that your mother-in-law give a party to celebrate your marriage after the wedding trip, for example.

Miss Manners gathers that instead, this lady was merely assigned the night before the wedding and is trying to make the most of it. For the sake of your future family relations, she urges you to work out a compromise that will recognize the legitimacy of her wanting to include her friends, without harping too much on the awkward way she has been trying to accomplish this.

Inviting the Attendants

DEAR MISS MANNERS—Should a wedding invitation be sent out to members of the bridal party? Or is this redundant, since the best man, maid of honor, etc., have all been "invited" to the wedding already?

GENTLE READER—Miss Manners was entering into a legalistic debate with herself over whether the informally made, but highly personal, invitation to participate in a wedding made the formal invitation superfluous when she had the sense to step back a moment and look at the human element.

Wedding invitations are pretty souvenirs (at least the ones that aren't revoltingly cute) as well as reminders of the time and place of the wedding. Miss Manners cannot see any advantage in grudging the members of the wedding party either. Not even saving the cost of the stamps.

Strangers

UNKNOWN RELATIVES

DEAR MISS MANNERS—Is it proper to send a wedding invitation to first cousins whom I've never met? I would like to get to know them and want them to come to my wedding, if at all possible. Should a personal note be included with the invitation, explaining how we are related?

GENTLE READER—You are going to have to explain more than that, Miss Manners is afraid. You are going to have to explain why you never thought of getting to know them before and how you plan to do so, while presumably tending to other matters, on your wedding day.

THE BULLETIN-BOARD INVITATION

DEAR MISS MANNERS—At the small community church we attend each Sunday, with seventy to eighty people, a trend we find offensive has recently been started. One invitation is sent, addressed to the church congregation, and is read aloud from the pulpit to those in attendance, and then posted at the back of the church. No one who attends our church is sent a personal invitation. This is even being done by our pastor's children. What do you make of this, and what should our response be? We realize that invitations are expensive, but it doesn't seem like a good area to cut back on these expenses.

GENTLE READER—Always looking for a kindly interpretation, Miss Manners is assuming that these invitations are not intended to replace individual ones sent to friends. Rather, she hopes, they are there to re-enforce the traditional notion that public ceremonies are—well, public. Anyone in a congregation is therefore welcome to attend weddings or other ceremonies held in the church.

It would be not only rude, but unwise in the extreme, to use this procedure for a private social event, such as a wedding reception.

Bulletin-board invitations do not obligate unnamed people to observe the usual conventions, such as replying to invitations and sending presents. Nor should they entitle those anonymous people to attend anything but the ceremony itself, in their capacity of being members of the same congregation. Miss Manners would have very little sympathy for anyone who omitted the individual invitations to related festivities. She wouldn't quite snicker at the empty—or overcrowded—receptions that are likely to result because she doesn't enjoy other people's discomfort even when it is deserved. But she would rejoice that for once, the failure of anyone to perform the duties of invited guests would be no fault of the guests.

The "And" Crowd

DEAR MISS MANNERS—A bride-to-be who is a sixth-grade teacher wants to invite her students, age ten to twelve years old, to her wedding. They do not drive or date. Should the envelope read "Miss (or Mr.) Student and parents?" If the parent is single and his/her date is included, how is the wording changed? Should the inner envelope be worded the same?

GENTLE READER—The rule is that wedding guests may only be invited by name, and never mind how often this rule is violated. Adding "and parents," along with all the other And People—And Family, And Guest, And Escort— may indicate tolerance for other people's appendages, but stops short of hospitality. Rather, it makes clear that the hosts don't much care to bother finding out who these people actually are. In each case, there is someone obvious to ask for the name, which can then be put on the invitation, so that everyone who attends gets the full guest treatment. The bride's students can tell her the names of their parents and they at least know where to go to find out the names of a single parent's current partner.

Miss Manners has another suggestion, however. Having brought up the subject of hospitality, she will not actually discourage the bride from swelling her guest list by multiplying the class size times three. But invitations to students only, with a card to the parents advising them when and where the children can be dropped off and picked up, would add to their sense of privilege in being invited to the wedding.

'n' Guest . . .

DEAR MISS MANNERS— I am from a small, midwestern town, where we invite friends to weddings, not friend 'n' escorts or escortees. Here, it is different. Persons who attend weddings are assumed to need the security of a partner in order to celebrate the event—even if that person is a complete stranger to the bride and groom.

This is repulsive to me. I do not want outsiders at my wedding. I consider it an intimate ceremony, which is not to be thrown open to casual inspection. How can I get around the trend? I don't want to offend my friends or have them think my motivation is financial. Can we get away with leaving "and guest" off invitations?

GENTLE READER—Miss Manners knew you and she would get along when she saw that " 'n,' " which not only acknowledges that letters are missing on both sides of the 'n,' but seems to hold that mutilated conjunction with pincers. So of course you also understand how outrageous it is for wedding guests to expect to be able to bring casual dates to such a momentous occasion as a wedding. However, guests should properly be invited to bring their spouses, fiancés, or whatever passes for such if one doesn't inquire too closely; those people are prospective friends, rather than absolute strangers.

The offense to guests, as well as to hosts, is in that phrase "and guest," which may be translated as, "oh, just anyone." What you should do is to ask those guests of whose personal lives you have lost track if they are attached, and if so, to whom. Then send invitations to those people by name.

What do you say if a guest asks to bring a friend? Well, you have a choice:

1. "How delightful. We'd love to meet him."

or

2. "I'm so sorry, but we're only asking people we know to our wedding; but we'd be delighted to meet him on another occasion."

"Real" Guests

DEAR MISS MANNERS—I went to a formal wedding as the guest of a friend—I didn't know the bride or the groom, but the groom had invited my friend to bring a guest. After the ceremony, the bride stood on a stairway and threw her bouquet out into the room. I was near the front of the group and as the bouquet came right to me, I caught it. The bridesmaids were standing behind me with their arms outraised, but I didn't know it.

My friend says I shouldn't have done that—or at least that I should have given it back, or given it to one of the bridesmaids, as the bride had intended for one of them to catch it. Did I commit a social blunder?

GENTLE READER—The social blunder, Miss Manners keeps trying to teach people who won't listen, is right there in the wedding invitation addressed to "and guest" or "and escort." Your experience is an example of how it creates the unspeakable result of having first- and second-class guests. You were chastised because you weren't considered a "real" guest—a hideously rude concept violating all traditions of hospitality.

(Warning: Tirade immediately ahead. Be back with the bouquet aspect when it's over.)

Miss Manners is all for inviting wedding guests to come as couples—indeed, there is a new rudeness of inviting only half of a married couple, which she is trying to stamp out. Those who are married, engaged, or otherwise firmly attached should be asked to social events (as opposed to office gatherings, which are still office gatherings, no matter how many drinks are served) in tandem. Strictly optionally, but if the hosts are feeling generous, or lonely, they can ask their guests if there is someone they would like to bring, find out that person's name, and issue another invitation. But no one should be expected to surrender control of the guest list to the guests themselves, allowing them to bring strangers. Having done that, however, they are obliged to treat all their guests equally graciously.

Bridesmaids are considered to be entitled to the choice positions for catching the bridal bouquet, but the custom allows all unmarried female guests to participate.

Not Unless He's Related

DEAR MISS MANNERS—I know columnists receive gag letters, but believe me, this is not one! The parents of one of our daughter's bridesmaids have a monkey which they are training to help care for a paraplegic. They take the animal with them when they go out. They have threatened not to attend the wedding because we did not include the monkey on their invitation.

I do not feel that a monkey belongs at as solemn an occasion as a wedding. It chatters continually and bangs around its cage. Also, there will be children in attendance, and I fear they will be bitten. I think what they are doing is admirable, but is it unreasonable to ask them to leave the monkey in the care of others on this special day? My daughter does not want it, either, but is reluctant to press the point because she wants to continue to be friends with the daughter and will have to see the parents on occasion. How can we graciously let them know our concerns?

GENTLE READER—Well, let's see. Miss Manners has been riffling through the files she keeps right behind her august forehead, and has not succeeded in finding anything under Monkeys, Undesirable as Guests. But let's do a bit of cross-file checking here. How about the rule saying that wedding guests may not bring along their own, uninvited guests? That should take care of it.

No?

All right, here's one under Animals, Working. It says that trained assistance animals, such as Seeing Eye dogs, may go anywhere their owners do. But this monkey is not yet trained and, not being in attendance on one of the guests, would be there in a social and not a working capacity.

You are quite right to suspect that monkeys who are solely out for a good time do not make ideal guests, although Miss Manners wouldn't count on the children's not having a better time than they suspected possible. To inform the guests of your decision, you might adapt the general rule formed for excluding children—"We are so sorry that we can't have your darling monkey, who would undoubtedly behave beautifully, but we feel we just can't make an exception because other people might want to bring theirs, who might not behave as well."

8

THE INVITATION
AND ANNOUNCEMENT

What do you want your wedding guests to do with your invitations after they receive them?

Well, yes, it might be a nice idea if they answered them. Perhaps they might also want to carry them around, in order to have the address handy when they spot a silver tea service that would look darling in your new studio apartment. They could then file the invitation in the household calendar, so that they showed up at the right time and place. After that—okay, they're probably not going to have them bronzed.

What you don't want them to do is to forward them to Miss Manners with the indignant notation "Will you look at THAT!?!" written across your lovingly joined names. Yet people do that. And these are not finicky cranks like Miss Manners, who can tell real engraving from raised print, no matter how solemnly your printer swore that would be impossible. (Nevertheless, polite people are much too overcome with pleasure at the prospect of other people's happiness to enjoy a small sneer when people save the money of engraving by sending faked engraving, instead of even cheaper, but frank and honest, printing, or invitations written by hand.)

By far the largest category of invitations submitted for Miss Manners' disapproval are actually attempts to shake down the wedding guests, either by charging them or suggesting that they take over the couple's shopping for them. So much for the idea that rudeness is just an unfortunate symptom of unhappiness, while bliss inspires courtesy.

Other invitations that their recipients find distasteful are not ill meant. They are, to be sure, attempts to pull off a fast one, but for convenience, rather than profit. They are wrong answers to the question of "How can you treat people like wedding guests without actually having them as wedding guests?" (The right answer is, "You can't.")

The most original example sent Miss Manners (and "original," in the etiquette trade, is generally not a compliment) was a formally worded one from a couple who gave themselves "the distinct pleasure of announcing our marriage. Our life together began in a private church ceremony consisting of just the two of us. Although your presence would have been a blessing and an honour, we ask for your continued thoughts and prayers."

Now, a wedding announcement is a perfectly respectable item of social correspondence. No apologies are made for not including the person at the wedding; the fact of the marriage is simply conveyed, after it has happened, and it calls for nothing more than a note of congratulation. This, with its unconvincing insinuation that the couple was somehow forcibly prevented from inviting guests, is a non-invitation rather than an announcement. The person who received it reported "a distinct lack of pleasure" in reading it.

Miss Manners trusts that it was a hideous mix-up of some sort and not similar to the attempt, described by a gentleman who reports: "On Tuesday, we received an invitation to the wedding of a friend's daughter—a wedding that turned out to have been the previous Saturday. I said to my

MR. AND MRS. GREATLY RELIEVED

HAVE THE HONOR OF ANNOUNCING

THE MARRIAGE OF THEIR DAUGHTER

DARLING AIRHEAD

TO

MR. ORVILLE SUITABLE RIGHT

ON SATURDAY, THE FIRST OF APRIL

ST. JUDE THE OBSCURE CHURCH

LOOKOUT, MARYLAND

Although mean-spirited people try to claim that a wedding announcement is really a request for a wedding present from those who have not attended the wedding, this is an improper thought. A wedding announcement is the announcement that a wedding has taken place. The response to it should be a letter of congratulations.

wife, 'Well, we missed that one; what a pity. The invitation must have been delayed in the mail.' But then we looked at the postmark and it had been mailed on Monday. Why would anyone be sending out wedding invitations two days after the wedding?"

Perhaps the senders did not understand that you cannot use invitations for announcements (see above). If the thought was that those who were not invited would be nevertheless flattered to receive an invitation, presumably to cherish as a souvenir of an event from which they were excluded, it was not a good idea.

Then there is the lady who wants the wedding guests, only providing she doesn't have to get married: "My granddaughter, a twenty-five-year-old schoolteacher, has been living with a man sixteen years her senior, who has a son twelve years old. He has just closed a bar he operated and is apparently heavily in debt. They are planning a large fake wedding—nothing legal, everything as if it were the real thing—because she wants to have a baby, but thinks if she is legally married to him, she will become responsible for his debts. Maybe I am too old-fashioned, but my husband and I refuse to go."

Yes, you two and Miss Manners are hopelessly old-fashioned in believing that wedding guests ought to be genuine guests invited to a genuine wedding. She suspects that the rest of the world has not progressed either to the point of enjoying being socially duped.

A Do-It-Yourself Invitation

DEAR MISS MANNERS—We are having a wedding for my daughter and her fiancé at 3:30, with a reception afterward at the church with finger food, cake, and punch. That night, around 7 P.M., we plan to go to a restaurant where a band plays and the bride and groom can dance. How can

Mr. and Mrs. Greatly Relieved

request the honor of your presence

at the marriage of their daughter

Darling Airhead

to

Mr. Orville Suitable Right

on Saturday, the first of April

at twelve o'clock

St. Jude the Obscure Church

and afterwards at

The Lookout Inn

Lookout, Maryland

R.s.v.p.

Now that we consider it outrageous to invite some people to depart after the ceremony while inviting others to stay for the wedding cake and champagne, this is the standard invitation to a wedding and a wedding breakfast, reception, or dinner. A separate reception card could be used with an invitation to the ceremony, just as *u* could be added to *honor*, but this is not necessary.

It is no accident that there is no form for that abomination, the response card. "R.s.v.p." is quite enough of a concession. It should not be necessary to alert anyone of sense and good will that it is obligatory to answer such an invitation, and if the guests can't figure out where to write, they can check the return address on the envelope we correctly invite guests to come join us there for eating or dancing, to watch the bride and groom dancing, and let them know that any expenses will be theirs? In other words, we would like for many of the guests to come join in the celebration, but cannot afford to pay the bill for everyone to eat or drink.

GENTLE READER—There is no correct way to issue an invitation for people to take themselves out to dinner, and Miss Manners is afraid that providing entertainment in the form of allowing them to watch a newly married couple dancing doesn't change that.

You can try to instill in them a desire to keep partying after the reception is over by running around the reception telling them, breathlessly, where you are all going later, and adding, as if spontaneously, "It would be fun if you went, too." Just don't blame Miss Manners if they have so much fun that they all decide to go along for the next stop, as well.

Handwritten Invitations

DEAR MISS MANNERS—I am planning a wedding for this spring and since my budget is not unlimited, I would like to know if hand-printed invitations (calligraphy) would be acceptable. I would still use formal style—the cards just wouldn't be professionally engraved. Would this upset people who received them?

GENTLE READER—Miss Manners hesitates to say what would upset some people nowadays, but anyone who took your plan amiss would have an upside-down sense of propriety. Engraving is the proper way of imitating handwriting for the convenience of large mailings of formal invitations. A bride who did have an unlimited budget might well consider having her invitations done by hand instead.

Dear Sally and Jack,

    Brendan and I are getting married on Saturday, the second of June, at two o'clock here in our roof garden. We very much want you to come and stay afterwards to help us celebrate.

                Fondly yours,
                Harriett.

An informal wedding invitation is just as proper as a formal one provided that the informality is achieved honestly, with a letter, rather than by messing up the formal form (omitting honorifics, adding hearts and flowers, using nauseating phrases referring to the couple's sentiments for each other, or adding other unattractive or embarrassing "personal" touches) or by using faked engraving.

Mr. and Mrs. Frank Lee Baffled

request the honour of your presence

at the marriage of their daughter

Camilla Madeline

Captain, United States Army

to

Duong Tran Awful-Nuisance

Lieutenant, United States Army

on Saturday, the twentieth of December

at two o'clock

Old Post Chapel

Camp Dusseldorf, Germany

Reception

immediately following the ceremony

Camp Dusseldorf Officers Club

R.s.v.p.
APO 1234
New York, New York

Admiral Stacey Awful-Nuisance

Major General Trevor Nuisance

request the honour of your presence

at the marriage of

Camilla Madeline Baffled

Captain, United States Army

to their son

Duong Tran

Lieutenant, United States Army

on Saturday, the twentieth of December

at two o'clock

Old Post Chapel

Camp Dusseldorf, Germany

The European-style invitation is another solution to the complaint that the bridegroom's parents are omitted from the traditional invitation (because they weren't the hosts, because everybody knew them, because they lived next door to the bride's parents, and because nobody much cared about the male side of the event).

Multiple Parents

DEAR MISS MANNERS—When the parents of a child are divorced and one or both has remarried, does the child now have three or four parents, or does he continue having only the original two?

I have read many announcements where the parents are listed as follows: "Mr. and Mrs. John Jones and Mrs. Mary Jones" (where mother has not remarried); "Mr. and Mrs. John Jones and Mr. and Mrs. James Smith"; or "Mr. John Jones and Mrs. Mary Smith."

With all the remarrying of today, doesn't the child still have only two parents? (Deceased parents are a totally different issue.)

GENTLE READER—When it comes to distributing parents among children, Miss Manners is inclined to be generous. Her own dear mother—she only had one—was a teacher, and she used to be pleased when all sorts of adults, including former stepparents no longer married to a parent of origin, continued to take an interest in a child. So while the announcements you mention are socially cumbersome, Miss Manners is not going to condemn them.

Convictions

DEAR MISS MANNERS—I want to word my wedding invitations so as to include the women's names in an acceptable way without bowing down too much to tradition. It is important to me that women are not referred to as "Mrs. His Name" (first and last) because I believe that such wording, no matter how formal, implies not only that married women are unequal to their husbands, but also that married women are not important in their own right—that their identities are subsumed by the identity of the husband.

I have in mind having the names of both my parents and my stepparents at the top as "Adam Ray and Sharon Magnum with John Wesley and Susan Hearn Doe." I would prefer not to use the phrase "the parents of" as a way of avoiding the issue, because all of the people to be mentioned on the invitation are very important to me, will be paying substantially for the wedding and deserve to have their full names acknowledged.

GENTLE READER—Please allow Miss Manners gently to suggest that before one attempts to improve upon tradition, perhaps one should find out what that tradition is. Two points that you seem to have missed are that honorifics are used on formal invitations (but not "parents of") and that people should be consulted about how they wish to style themselves.

Never mind your arguments about how you think other people should be addressed, unless the ladies in question share them. If they do, the correct formal honorific before their full names is "Ms." If they do not, they should be styled Mr. and Mrs. In so personal a matter as a name, your convictions do not properly apply to people who do not share them.

The Invitation from Beyond

DEAR MISS MANNERS—I received an invitation that read: "Janet Smith and Dr. John Jones, deceased, request the honor of your presence at the wedding of their daughter . . ." (Incidentally, the mother has remarried since the death of Dr. Jones.)

GENTLE READER—It is not an uncommon impulse to want to treat the dead as if they were alive, and this particular kind of attempt to resurrect a parent for a wedding always breaks Miss Manners's heart.

Less tenderhearted people only break up with laughter. "He's dead!" they exclaim; "so just exactly where does he want our presence?" It is no honor to subject one's parent's name to such creepy usage. Only the living can issue invitations. This one should have been from "Ms. Janet Smith" or "Mr. and Mrs. Jeremiah Newhusband" requesting "the honor of your presence at the marriage of her daughter."

The Enclosures

What's this fat, unsolicited envelope in your mail, packed with forms that you must fill out and instructions that you must obey?

Did you forget that you put yourself on the waiting list of a college that is now suffering from post–baby-boom depression and has decided to admit you, after all?

Was the national draft reinstituted without your having heard about it, and have you been ordered up to serve your country?

Miss Manners can reassure you—somewhat. You have only been invited to a wedding by people who have gone around the bend.

Out of a frenzied desire to be helpful, or perhaps out of an insane attack of bossiness, these people are mailing you a package of options and orders that is second only to the federal income tax form in its bewildering complexity.

You have here:

Flight information, group rates at hotels, babysitting services, and valet parking validation.
Admonitions about not smoking, not arriving late, and not wearing colors that would conflict with the theme of the bridal party.

Mr. and Mrs. Samuel McGee

1 Marge Drive
Lake Lebarge, Alaska   78877

Ms. Heidi Megabyte

Mr. and Mrs. Theodore Bishop Right

request the honour of your presence

at the marriage of their daughters

Lauren Whitney

to

Mr. Maxwell Scott Nicely

and

Heather Brittany

to

Mr. Daniel Service McGee

on Saturday, the second of June

at six o'clock

Our Lady of Propriety Church

and at a reception

following the ceremony

The Bideawhile Hotel

Brookdale Connecticut

R.s.v.p.
129 Primrose Path
Brookdale, Connecticut   01110

Complications in the marital lives of the parental generation have been handled
in this double-wedding invitation by having the mother, father, and stepmother of
the two brides as hosts, while the parents of one of the bridegrooms have slipped
their own card into the invitations sent to their side of the family to avoid their
friends' exclaiming, "Who on earth are these people?"

The pleasure of your company

is requested at the marriage of

Dr. Harriett Grundy

to

Mr. Brendan Truly Repellent

on Saturday, the thirteenth of October

at four o'clock

Baronial Baroque Hotel

New York City

and afterwards at a reception

R.s.v.p.
29 Alimentary Canal
New York, NY 10014

A couple giving its own wedding modestly goes into the passive tense when issuing formal invitations.

Directions on how to get there, and predictions about what the weather is likely to be.

Hints, and not too subtle ones, about how to make the occasion materially rewarding to the bridal couple.

A fill-in-the-blanks response card with a mysterious M—— and a line on which you apparently may indicate how large an entourage you have.

A deadline for answering the invitation, along with a threat in case you fail to comply with it.

A menu from which to select your dinner, or an order to bring a dish for everyone to eat, or a warning that there will be a charge for drinks.

Suggestions about what else to do with your time when it is not being occupied with the wedding or related events.

To those who just want to push all that junk off their desks and forget the whole thing, Miss Manners cannot offer relief. She can only plead with their prospective hosts not to inundate them with unnecessary, much less impertinent, material.

Most traditional enclosure cards are no longer used. A ceremony card enclosed with a reception invitation, or a reception card with a ceremony invitation, means that not all wedding guests were invited to both, a distinction that is bound to cause insult nowadays. Cards of admission imply that you expect your wedding to be crashed, which may be a reach unless you are a movie star or the president's daughter.

At-home cards, which give the couple's post-wedding address, do not go into invitations, but into wedding announcements. (Then they are highly useful, because, although the address may seem superfluous if the couple has been living together for years, they show the couple's choice of surnames.)

The address to which wedding invitation replies are to be directed should be that on the back of the envelope. And this brings Miss Manners to the distasteful question of enclosed response cards, with or without their own self-addressed envelopes cunningly decorated with a "Love" stamp.

It's not just that any response cards are not-quite-nice because decent people of course already know (yes? yes?) that they must always reply to invitations. The sad fact is that for indecent people, cards are not going to help. Just as many cases of unmailed response cards are reported as other unanswered invitations, so you might as well save the expense and trouble of enclosing them.

Miss Manners does admit the usefulness of enclosing instruction cards with invitations to out-of-the-way places. Other well-meaning information, such as transportation possibilities and deals and other recreational opportunities, should be conveyed informally, in separate letters to guests who accept the invitation.

Beyond that, the wedding planners will simply have to trust their guests to behave themselves and perhaps to fork over something the couple might like. Miss Manners is not guaranteeing that they will do this without instruction—they are your friends, not hers—but only pointing out that nagging is as rude as it probably is useless.

Parking Enclosure

DEAR MISS MANNERS—We wish to pay for the guests' valet parking at the elegant downtown hotel where our daughter's wedding and reception will be held. How do we indicate to our guests that they are to inform the parking attendants that they are attending the wedding? We cannot get parking tickets in advance. May we design some sort of enclosure card to be presented to the parking attendants? What wording would you suggest?

GENTLE READER—On the waste-not-want-not principle, Miss Manners has delved into her box of leftover traditional forms and come up with the enclosure card designed to tell the guests that a special train had been hired to take them to the wedding. There was a lot of dust on it. Here is the new version:

> *Special parking facilities will be available.*
> *Please show this card at the entrance.*

Bridal Registry Card

DEAR MISS MANNERS—My sister is to be married, and the department store she registered with gave her 600 registry cards to put in all 600 formal wedding invitations. When I was married, it was my understanding that the proper etiquette was to place bridal registry cards in bridal shower invitations only.

Has etiquette changed, as my sister states? She is having four bridal showers and is inviting fifty women to each—200 people. Should she include the cards both in their shower and wedding invitations?

GENTLE READER—Where is your family getting its information? Etiquette hadn't even changed to what you thought it was when you got married, let alone to what your sister seems to think. It has always been rude to notify guests what you want to receive as a present or where you want them to buy it, and it always will be. The only use of bridal registry cards that Miss Manners authorizes is as scratch paper for the bride.

Tissue Paper

DEAR MISS MANNERS—When sending wedding invitations, what is the explanation of the white silk paper inside the card? When we received the invitation cards that we ordered, there was no silk paper.

GENTLE READER—Silk paper? Did the bride get her veil caught in the invitations? Oh, you mean the tissue paper. That is there so that the engraving doesn't get smudged when it is fresh. By the time you get all those addresses written, you don't need to worry about that. Nevertheless, some people keep the tissue in when they send out the invitation just to prove that it is really engraved. Miss Manners considers that to be like keeping the store cellophane on the lampshade to show that it's of good material.

Double Envelopes

DEAR MISS MANNERS—Why do wedding invitations come inside two envelopes? Wouldn't one be sufficient?

GENTLE READER—Well, a postcard would be sufficient to convey the information, if it comes down to that. The tradition of using two envelopes simulates the old hand-delivered message, combining it with the utilitarian necessity of its being sent by mail.

Miss Manners is making that up. Rational explanations of old customs are always supplied after the fact, not so much to explain what has been lost in time as to disguise the fact that customs are rarely logical. But arguments of paper waste have penetrated this custom before. During World War II, an unfolded wedding invitation, measuring

4½ by 6 inches, was used in a single envelope, and Miss Manners invites you to take advantage of this less venerable tradition.

Addressing

DEAR MISS MANNERS—I am a calligrapher and have been asked to address wedding invitations, both outside and inside envelopes. What is the proper way to word the various situations that arise? There are so many different ways of living together, and each person having different titles.

GENTLE READER—There sure are different ways of living together these days, and Miss Manners doesn't want to hear about some of them. All that concerns her, and you, is that people who live in the same household may get joint invitations, but may need to have separate lines for their names. If, for any reason, simple joint honorifics ("Mr. and Mrs.," "The Misses Doe," "The Doctors Roe") cannot be used, then put each full name with its proper honorific on a separate line on the outside envelope, and each honorific and surname on a separate line on the inside envelope.

When to Mail

DEAR MISS MANNERS—Weddings are very special, and dates and places seem to be firm months before the event. Is it permissible to send out invitations six weeks before the wedding? This would permit family and friends to respond, make travel plans and somewhat compensate for poor mail service.

GENTLE READER—Indeed, Miss Manners has decreed that four to six weeks prior to the wedding is proper in this age of scattered families and discounted air fares. The traditionally shorter period assumed that the bride and bridegroom met across the fence between their houses, and the neighbors had been watching the whole courtship from the porch.

At-Home Cards

DEAR MISS MANNERS—I am a born feminist soon to marry into a family with very traditional attitudes. This family has a large like-minded social group. Recently, my fiancé and I were introduced at a retirement party as "This is John Doe and the future Jane Doe." In a flash of annoyance at the presumption that I would carry on a tradition deeply rooted in sexism, I responded tersely, "No, the forever-to-remain Jane Smith!" This exchange upset my future mother-in-law, who directed the question "Why are you getting married if she's not going to take your name?" to my fiancé, out of my hearing.

I do not wish to offend my future family and their friends when the issue arises, but it is difficult for me to keep my zeal on the subject in check. I realize there are forums more appropriate to such discussion than a formal banquet. How might I gracefully correct others who might make the error in the future? I would also like them to know that I am open for a discussion of the subject at another time.

GENTLE READER—It is not that Miss Manners does not sympathize with your desire to be addressed, in your future married life, as you wish to be. It's just that she has so much more sympathy for the poor lady who is about to acquire a zealous daughter-in law in search of forums to debate a personal decision.

A graceful way to let people know what your name will be after marriage is to enclose at-home cards with your wedding announcements with your and your husband's names on a line each, instead of as Mr. and Mrs., and to have paper made with your name, on which to write letters of

thanks for wedding presents and all the rest of your correspondence.

An ungraceful way is tersely to correct people who
make a simple mistake, based on years of tradition, and to
tax them with sexism for following social custom. Miss
Manners fails to see why you need open the matter for discussion. Are you not prepared to be as tolerant of other
ladies' choices as of your own?

The Poisoned Announcement

DEAR MISS MANNERS—A few years ago, I had a rather
nasty breakup with a young man to whom I had briefly
been engaged. I am now engaged again, to a wonderful
man. Could I send an announcement of my marriage this
winter to the previous man? Would that be perceived as
petty and unforgivable, or is it within etiquette's definition
of revenge? I would not want to step outside the bounds of
propriety.

GENTLE READER—What you are proposing to do is
within etiquette's definition of propriety, never mind
revenge. Wedding announcements are intended to be
sent to anyone you think might be interested to hear of
the marriage.

That settled, Miss Manners would like to discuss your
motive—not so much in terms of whether it is pleasant, but
of whether it has a chance of producing the effect you wish.
She asks you to consider that the gentleman on whom you
wish to wreak revenge would be perfectly within the
bounds of propriety to send you a letter in which he
expressed nothing but delight at your marriage—and that
he might even mean it. She therefore believes that you
would be better advised to concentrate your emotional
attentions on the wonderful gentleman to whom you are
now engaged.

MR. AND MRS. MAXWELL SCOTT NICELY

WILL BE AT HOME

AFTER THE FOURTH OF JULY

"FAUX CHATEAU"
1120806 HORSESHOE NAIL COURT
STEEPLECHASE, MARYLAND 20854

Ms. Heather Brittany Right-Megabyte

Mr. Daniel Service McGee

29 Alimentary Canal
Apartment 2-B
After the tenth of August   New York, New York 10014

One bride has decided to shock her mother by taking her new husband's name, while the other has seized the opportunity to add her mother's surname to her father's. Etiquette prudently keeps out of the way when these emotionally charged decisions are made, only asking that brides let their friends know what they wish to be called. The traditional at-home card, just the right size to tuck into an address book, nicely serves this purpose.

A Year Late

DEAR MISS MANNERS—My daughter just informed me that she was married a year ago. Do I send announcements now? Do I give her a reception now? Please advise me as soon as possible.

GENTLE READER—Miss Manners sees that you expect higher standards of promptness from her than you do from your daughter. A year is late to send formal wedding announcements, which are correctly mailed on the day of the wedding. Nor should you exactly give them a wedding reception. But by all means inform everyone who might be interested, through letters and telephone calls. It would also be nice to give a reception in honor of the couple, informing guests in a toast (rather than ahead of time on the invitations) of the occasion.

The Response

DEAR MISS MANNERS—My husband and I were married in a foreign country. When we returned home, we sent out announcements but did not have a reception. The responses we got from the announcements were varied. Could you please tell me what an appropriate response would have been (i.e., gift, cash, card, or a combination). We were not registered.

GENTLE READER—You got varied responses because you sent your announcements to a variety of people. That is as it should be and Miss Manners is not going to deal with any subtexts about feeling cheated out of loot. A wedding announcement requires only a letter of congratulation. However, people who are particularly close to and fond of the couple often take that opportunity to send a symbolic representation of their affection.

9

THE
FAMILY

Chief Duties of the Bride's Parents

1. Welcome the bridegroom to the family, and relieve his anxiety by telling him how they would now like him to address them.

2. Gently explain the facts of life to the bride: That the wedding must be within the financial capabilities and general style of the way the family lives, not a bankrupting fantasy; that the ordinary considerations of respect for parents, obligations of relationship and friendship for family and attendants, and concern for the comfort and pleasure of guests are not to be suspended; that marriage is supposed to be forever; and that yes, in this day and age, people still expect prompt handwritten thank-you letters.

3. Act as hosts to the extent agreed upon in family council with the bride (who must bear in mind that presiding is not indissolubly linked with paying): Planning the rehearsal, wedding reception, and any auxiliary entertaining;

issuing the invitations and announcements; arranging for the officiant, site, flowers, music, food and drink, transportation, and clothing of the bride and her attendants; and suggesting accommodations for the wedding party.

4. Restrain their own temptation to use the occasion to settle old scores, for example against each other's present spouses.

5. Veto black dresses or period costumes for the bridesmaids; head off any attempts by the bride to request showers or dictate wedding presents; remind the bride never to drink to herself when she is being toasted; and brief her on what to expect on her wedding night, if she does not have her own children to do this.

Chief Duties of the Bridegroom's Parents

1. Call on the bride's family (in person, if possible; otherwise by letter, E-mail being not formal enough for the occasion), propose a meeting, and declare how lucky they believe their son to be.

2. Keep up that tone, true or not, pronouncing everyone and everything perfectly lovely, while channeling any complaints they have about the arrangements through their son to the bride.

3. Supply an accurate copy of their guest list, without abbreviations or question marks, and keeping to the limit set, knowing that they can always give a party during the engagement or

after the marriage to introduce the bride to their hordes of friends.

4. Joke about how unfair it is that the bride's family has so much more to do than they, and offer to help out, usually by entertaining the bridal party, officiant, all their spouses, and, if possible, the out-of-town guests, the night before the wedding.

5. Spare the bride the necessity of reminding the bridegroom to buy her engagement and wedding rings, to let her know tactfully whether or not he would like a wedding ring, to get the license, to order the bridal bouquet and boutonnieres, to pay the officiant, to choose the best man and groomsmen, to talk them out of protesting about what they are expected to wear, to give them presents, and to throw the bachelor dinner, if they have not already planned one for him.

Chief Duties of Stepparents

1. Step into parental roles when invited to do so but refrain from sulking if not.

2. Maintain a graceful balance between parental pride and deference to birth parents, no matter how unworthy of honor they may be.

Money and Happiness

Clumping up and down the aisle, stalking the "Father of the Bride" and the other genial characters in the most recent version of the movie by that name, is the traditional American wedding curse. It is the firmly held notion that when a young woman falls in love, her parents will fall in debt.

Beneath a benevolent family story, the point is dramatically made that any wedding to which people attempt to apply the ordinary budgetary restraints appropriate to their circumstances will be pitiful and unmemorable. Parents who care for their daughters should not even hesitate to capitulate to such possibly ruinous demands as $1,200 wedding cakes and $250-a-head dinners, it argues. The mother of the bride makes the point that attention to prices spoils the bride's pleasure in her wedding.

Then the folly of doing so is demonstrated when the few limitations on expenditures or cheaper alternatives on which the father has insisted result in disaster. By not buying the most expensive clothes for himself, he has had a dark blue dinner jacket foisted off on him as black and is ridiculed by everyone, even the neighborhood policeman. That person is there to threaten the event because the other saving, having only two valet parking attendants instead of four, has induced presumably disgusted guests to leave their cars illegally blocking the street.

In this case, the family has enough money to propitiate demanding commercial interests. Both parents run successful businesses and, as the mother points out, they don't travel or indulge in other luxuries. So, in a tender scene when the father catches the daughter reading budget tips, he vows not to put her through the humiliation of a reasonably priced wedding.

It is not Miss Manners's function to save people money they want to spend. So she would have happily ignored all this, were it not for the heavy insinuation that the driving force behind all this is—poor old etiquette. Etiquette was portrayed as the villain—the handmaiden of commercialism, whose insidious ceremonial and emotional arguments always favored the spending of extravagant sums of money. It is made to seem rude to ask prices for commercial services and incorrect to limit wedding expenditures, even when they include planting tulips in the snow and making live swans waddle across the lawn.

Miss Manners is outraged. Etiquette does not practice extortion. Even the particular rules that were cited as required by wedding etiquette were totally false. Where did they get the claim that the bride's parents must pay the airfare of the bridegroom's foreign relatives? Never mind that his family was shown as richer than hers—transportation for relatives has never been a hostly obligation.

Midnight blue is the only color other than black that is, in fact, not considered vulgar for gentlemen's evening clothes. Its justification is the argument, made by highly fastidious gentlemen, that under artificial light, which is the only way evening clothes can be seen anyway, it looks blacker than black.

What Miss Manners resents most of all is the implication that in lesser circumstances—for example, in the only too common event that the parents' businesses happened to be suffering from the recession—the couple could not have had a beautiful and proper wedding. What a thoroughly improper idea *that* is.

Bill Paying

DEAR MISS MANNERS—I have just received the happy news that my eldest daughter is to be wed next year. In view of the fact that her mother and I are divorced, that I am remarried, and that the bride's mother is not, and further that her mother and I are both wage earners, I would appreciate your advice on the following matters.

1. Should the payment of the wedding be shared by both parents? Quite frankly, when I first considered this question, my initial reaction was that this was solely the obligation of the father. However, some similarly situated friends, both male and female, have suggested that there should be an equal sharing of costs. Other friends have said that depending on the financial position of the parties, there should be a division of cost wherein the father would bear more than fifty percent, and still others have even suggested that if the mother is unwilling to bear any of the cost, her relatives be excluded from the guest list unless she is willing to fund the cost attributable to their attendance.

2. In the event that it is your opinion that the mother should share in the expenses of the wedding, what, if any, changes would be mandated vis-à-vis the question of protocol; or, conversely, if the mother should not share in said expenses, what changes in protocol would you suggest?

It goes without saying that the happiness of the bride is paramount, since this is (hopefully) an once-in-a-lifetime experience. But many of my friends have indicated that the expense-sharing concept is realistic and fair, since although the father is the titular payor when the parents are still married, the other actually shares, since the money is derived from joint marital funds or indebtedness of both parents. This logic, to me, seems compelling.

GENTLE READER—Which would you prefer on this occasion, compelling logic or happiness of the bride? As you

declared the latter to be paramount, Miss Manners will try
to give you as much as possible of the former. Just don't
push her too far.

Etiquette says nothing about the vulgar idea of having
the financial backing of the wedding reflected in what you
call the protocol; it merely throws up its hands in horror.
The answer to your second question is: Don't even think
about it. The lady in question did not buy the position of
mother of the bride, and it cannot be withdrawn from her
for failure to pay wedding bills. Also, her relatives happen
also to be the bride's relatives, every single one of them.

As a matter of fact, etiquette, which messes around less
in the family budget than people seem to imagine, never
decreed that wedding bills were paid by the father of the
bride. Who signed the checks, whether there was a joint
account, and who brought what money to the parents' marriage were things about which etiquette minded its own
business. It merely said that the parents usually (but not
always) "gave" the wedding.

In the sweet old days that you imagine, the mother of
the bride (who may have been an heiress; did you think of
that?) did most of the "giving" because she did the planning. The bride, by standing at her side moaning, "Oh,
Mother," did her best to influence decisions, but the
mother was nominally in charge.

Now the balance of decision-making has been allowed
to shift to the bridal couple, even under the best of circumstances. When the parents are divorced, they should
try as best they can to make group decisions that will not
unduly burden or displease anyone. A family session in
which you all discuss the size and style of the wedding
would not be an inappropriate place for you to announce
that you would like to help realize the plans and to ask
your former wife tactfully what she would like to do.
Should she not be willing to contribute, you cannot

threaten to exclude her in any way, but you can—unless you magnanimously want to ignore the difference that it will make to you—enlist her and your daughter's help in figuring out how to scale down the wedding to what you can afford.

Bill Paying, Part Two

DEAR MISS MANNERS—Our son is to be married and the bride's parents have stated that it is proper for the groom's parents to pay for the flowers and the minister's services. We have never heard of this before. Have you?

GENTLE READER—Has your son perhaps heard of young men assuming financial responsibility when they get married? The relevant etiquette rule is that the bridegroom pays for the bridal bouquet and the wedding fee, not his parents. You may want to get this straightened out before someone tells you to go out and buy the bride a wedding ring.

The Family Meeting

DEAR MISS MANNERS—Please explain the duties of the groom's parents after the announcement of their son's engagement to a girl whose parents are divorced and unfriendly. I know it is our duty to have the girl's parents to our home. Should we have each parent over separately? Since we have briefly met each one, is it necessary to have them over at all?

GENTLE READER—Miss Manners hopes that you mean that the bride's parents are unfriendly to each other, not to you. She has an unpleasant picture of people whose response to "We're thrilled to hear that our son is to marry your lovely daughter" is a snarl.

In any case, you do want to do what you can to establish a friendly relationship with them. This is necessary on one level because etiquette requires that the bridegroom's parents create an occasion to tell the bride's parents how happy they are over the match. On another level, it is necessary because you need to establish a basis of sociability with people whose lives will be so much connected with yours over such matters as holidays and celebrations and grandchildren, should there be any. Two occasions to do this does not seem excessive to Miss Manners. Obviously, if they can't stand each other, it will not be a good idea to attempt to see them together.

The Night Before

What are you supposed to do the night before the wedding?

Oh, stop giggling. Nowadays, people don't even do that the night *of* the wedding, judging from the number of weary wedding guests who beg Miss Manners to let them off from the rule about staying at the wedding reception until the bridal couple leaves. Today's bridal couples aren't going anywhere while they still have anyone else left around to entertain them.

The problem of the night before the wedding is quite a different one. Then everyone wants to party. People who came in from out of town don't want to watch the cable movie in the hotel; they want to see who got invited and who got left out. The bridesmaids want to show everyone how good they can look when they choose their own clothes, instead of wearing that awful dress the bride chose, and they want to look over the groomsmen, who want to look over the bridesmaids. Reunited classmates want to find out what jobs their classmates got. Previously united relatives want to see how badly their replacements have aged. The bride's parents want to get away from all those planning books before they go stark-raving mad. Even the bride is torn between the desire not to have bags under her eyes the next day and the feeling that it's stupid to do nothing, especially if there is anyone in town who might otherwise be involved in a form of entertainment that does not feature her at its center.

This is clearly not a time to improvise. The planners of the wedding are so etiquette-logged by this time that they can't cross the street without looking up who should go first. There are so many relatives and friends available that to choose a few would inevitably insult others. So proper people look to tradition to tell them what to do. Then they have a problem. It happens that there are at least three traditions for the same night, involving most of the same people being at different events.

For example, there is the tradition of the bachelor party, and the more recent matching event, in which the bride and bridesmaids, in the noble name of equality, endeavor to out-vulgar the bridegroom and groomsmen.

Then there is the very old custom of the bride's parents' dinner, in which people who are already at the social and financial breaking point are forced to give a major dinner party the night before a major series of events at which they can't figure out how to use the same flowers. And there is the more recent tradition by which the bridegroom's parents give that dinner, which presents them with an opportunity to get even with the bride's family for allotting their side so few invitations to the wedding.

The idea of both parental dinners is twofold: To make sure that the wedding party attends the rehearsal, by tying up their evening; and to make sure the wedding comes off by tying up the evening of the bridal couple. Miss Manners attributes the continuing popularity of the last-night-out party for the bridegroom, and possibly also for the bride, to its stunning potential for outright disaster. One might presume that such a freedom-frolic would lose its zest for couples who have long been keeping house together, but perhaps its likelihood for creating a public cause of complaint between the couple actually adds some needed zest to the wedding itself. In contrast, the bride's parents' dinner would probably only strain the sanity of that couple and their relations with the new in-laws, which is why it has been pretty much dropped. For years, the bridegroom's family got off free financially, on the idea that their son would take over the sole support of the bride, but not even the bride believes in that any more.

An increasing sense that it is only fair for both families to be involved has made the bridegroom's parents' dinner the most usual pre–wedding-night custom now. It is the one that has Miss Manners's vote, since she is squeamish about attending weddings of families in the state of open hostility likely to result from the other options.

She cautions them to remember that they must be just as fastidious about it as if they had been undergoing the rigor that has been driving their counterparts nuts. They must include the spouses and para-spouses of the wedding party, and invite hardship cases—elderly relatives, people who have traveled for months to get there—unless other social provision for these people has been made. It is, everyone should remember, a time to be socially generous to those with whom you are about to become cemented, like it or not.

Stepfathers and Fathers

When Miss Manners hears about stepfathers, it is usually as their stepdaughters are about to trade them in. "Who should give me away?" they ask when they are planning to be married.

Well, dear, who has you? Never mind that it is usually the bridegroom. Miss Manners does not believe in spelling everything out on ceremonial occasions, even symbolically. Wedding guests are neither as innocent nor as easily titillated as young couples excitedly imagine.

The odd persistence of the archaic gesture of giving away a bride has often come to mean that on the threshold of starting her own married life, a young lady who has been reared and sheltered by a gentleman unrelated to her by blood will inquire how to explain to him that she is dividing the tasks of fatherhood—and that his lot is to pay bills, not to give her away.

Mind you, Miss Manners is not going to argue otherwise. It is true that the hosts of the wedding reception are responsible for providing refreshment for their guests, a point not to be taken for granted in the day of that abomination called the "cash bar." And the people whose names are on the top of the invitation are the hosts. (Surprise, surprise—you thought the bride and bridegroom were in charge, didn't you?) So if the bride's mother and her husband are giving the wedding, Miss Manners cannot relieve them of the responsibility of paying for whatever they (they!) decide they can afford.

Nor is Miss Manners opposed to having the bride's original father, or whatever we call such people nowadays (being referred to as biological parents sounds as if the act were performed for a science-fair demonstration) perform the charmingly anachronistic function of "giving her away" to a taker who may have already established as much possession as he can reasonably expect.

Finances aside, the bride's father is the bride's father. There may be circumstances that have made her feel that he has destroyed that tie, but otherwise it is the lot of kind stepparents to yield gracefully to prior claims, rather than to force her to make a wrenching choice. That said, Miss

Manners hopes those stepdaughters will take into account what a beautiful thing it is for someone to parent another person's child. Or to consider that family participation in a wedding is not a matter of casting preset roles, but of arranging things to fit the particular families involved.

For this reason, Miss Manners was delighted, rather than shocked, at the Gentle Reader who "couldn't pass up an opportunity to tell you about my granddaughter's wedding. She was 'given away' by four fathers!

"One was her stepfather, one was her natural father (who had been divorced when she was an infant and whom she had located a year or so before the wedding), one was my husband, who is her grandfather, and who had always been there for her while she was growing up, and one was the grandfather she had just found, her natural father's father. The murmurs and looks on the faces of the guests in the church would have made a hilarious movie. What exactly is important, anyway? To me, this was her way of expressing her love and her appreciation of the 'fathers' in her life."

The correct answer is, of course, that love is important. But Miss Manners, who also finds tradition important, is as charmed and amused as the guests. It is not exactly traditional to have four fathers give a bride away, but if the tradition is adapted to the family, rather than the other way around, this bride ends up with a nontraditional quartet of fathers. Miss Manners is not making this a general recommendation—you have to have a family, and friends, who have as much good nature and humor as this bride's grandmother. She just prefers to deal with questions of how to confer honor on stepfathers, rather than those on how to make them just quietly pay.

When the choice is made and explained tactfully, it behooves the one not chosen to be graceful. A bride who tells her stepfather that she loves him dearly but feels she should have her father with her, or one who explains to her father that she loves him dearly but her stepfather was the one with whom she grew up, should be met with an example of magnanimous acceptance.

If the Stepfather Gives Away the Bride, the Father . . .

DEAR MISS MANNERS—What is the proper role of the father of the bride when the bride chooses her stepfather to walk her down the aisle? There is no estrangement between father and daughter and he has provided financial and emotional support from infancy through college. The bride simply feels closer to her stepfather, having lived with him and her mother almost all her life. Surely the father's role does not just become that of a guest. But I have heard no alternative offered that would give an honored role to the father at the wedding and/or reception.

GENTLE READER—The proper role of the father in these circumstances is to beam. He must project this beam so that no one has any excuse for believing that his daughter or her stepfather has slighted him, or that he is miffed at either of them.

He may certainly be in the receiving line, if the stepfather and the father of the bridegroom are; if they choose to circulate as hosts instead, he may do the same. This consists of welcoming guests, seeing to it that no one is stranded, and confessing to them that he can hardly imagine his little girl is old enough to be married.

Presuming there is no animosity among different parts of the family, he should be seated with the other parents at the wedding breakfast. He may so assume—not necessarily exclusively—such fatherly privileges as offering a toast to the couple, enjoying an early dance with the bride, and enjoining the bridegroom to take good care of her.

Giving Away Mother

DEAR MISS MANNERS—My daughter, who is thirty-five, is having a large second wedding and has informed me she wants her two sons, age eighteen and eleven, to give her away, so that they will be part of the ceremony and not feel left out.

Where does this leave her father? We are a loving family and she loves her father very much, but she said he gave her away at the first wedding. Shouldn't the boys be ushers, or the eleven-year-old a ring bearer (or is he too old for that)?

GENTLE READER—Although Miss Manners admires the motivation for featuring children in a wedding that will make them part of a new family, she has to say that the symbolism of having a bride given away by her own children is not good. Far from leaving them for her new husband, as she does her father, she is taking them with her.

As for her father, she has already left his household, and the symbolism of his giving her away a second time is not great, either. It looks as though he plans to keep doing this until he finds a permanent taker. A wedding can be just as legal and charming when that particular ceremony is omitted. She can be escorted to the altar by her sons or her father, anyway, and, especially in a case such as yours, where feelings might be hurt, simply have him or them stand at the altar with her, as she takes her vows.

This might be better for the sons, anyway. On the one hand, they should not be left out, but on the other, they may not be as eager to acquire this new relative as their mother is, and should be allowed to participate without solemnly and publicly taking part in making it come about.

Stepmothers and Mothers

DEAR MISS MANNERS—My husband's daughter is getting married and I want to do what is best for all. I have told my stepdaughter that I will give her a bridal shower for her father's side of the family.

Am I supposed to invite her mother and grandmother? How am I to dress for the wedding day? Do I dress as though I'm the mother of the bride? Should the color of my dress match the bridesmaids' dresses? Do I wear a corsage? Where do I sit in church?

Is my husband also expected to have pictures taken with his ex-wife? Are my parents to be considered as grandparents? (My stepdaughter does not call them grandma and grandpa, but Mr. and Mrs.) My husband and his ex-wife divorced on unfriendly terms and he and I have been married for three years. What about when the bridal party is called to the dance floor and then the parents—is my husband expected to dance with his ex-wife? Or do I?

GENTLE READER—You certainly are not expected to dance with your husband's ex-wife. Miss Manners is happy to be able to provide you with instant relief from that worry. She can also get you off the shower hook, so to speak, if it is not too late. Showers are not supposed to be given by relatives of the guest of honor. You are her stepmother, and may give a luncheon or reception in her honor, but not a shower, because the last is characterized by the giving of presents and one is not supposed to be greedy on behalf of a relative. (See The Shower, page 65.)

As for the other activities—costuming the relatives, deciding the dance order and posing for pictures—these are not, repeat not, part of the proper wedding tradition. There is nothing wrong with consulting about clothing so that no one seriously clashes in style with anyone else; with wearing flowers; with signing up the bride for early dances with her closest male relatives; with having pictures taken. But these are not proper wedding rituals. There is no rule of etiquette mandating that mothers of the bride and bridegroom match anyone, even each other; there is no rule that certain female relatives must be distinguished with corsages; there is no rule that certain people must dance together, or must appear together in photographs.

There is a rule that everyone must be polite to everyone else, no matter what the previous family activities. This may very well mean pretending that they don't dislike one another, but it does not extend to pretending that the original couple are still married. The lady accompanying the father of the bride is his wife, not his former wife. Brides who wish to display such a charade at their wedding must be gently discouraged.

Gargoyles

DEAR MISS MANNERS—My stepson is going to be married this spring. My husband's two ex-wives will be there. Am I required to speak or be civil to these gargoyles? The wedding is going to be a small home wedding, so there will be no graceful way of avoiding the two.

GENTLE READER—Absolutely, Miss Manners requires that you be civil and speak to all the guests at the wedding. Unless, of course, your object is to inform everyone present that your husband is in the unfortunate habit of marrying nothing but gargoyles.

Unapproved Relatives

DEAR MISS MANNERS—Who should wear corsages at my son's traditional wedding to a very sweet girl? My mother passed away and my daddy soon remarried. An argument between me and him caused problems with other members of the family and my son and his fiancée do not speak to his grandfather very much. When they are around, you can feel the tension in the air, and they also feel not welcomed down their house. My son does not consider this woman his grandmother.

My daddy will wear a corsage at the wedding, as being a grandparent. Should his wife wear one? If she should, can it be a different kind than the rest of the wedding party? If she does, is my son acknowledging her as his grandmother?

GENTLE READER—Corsages are not legally binding. They should not even be as symbolically significant as they have become, but Miss Manners despairs of making people understand what an unfortunate idea it is to pin signs on some guests to signify that they are more important than others. Among other things, it leads to such potentially explosive situations as you describe.

Since you are politely overlooking family animosities to decorate the grandfather (with a single flower at the lapel, rather than a bouquet, Miss Manners trusts), you might as well go whole hog, if we can use that term in relation to politeness, and decorate his wife as well. Just don't search the plant world to try to make it clear that you are labeling her as second class.

Former Relatives

DEAR MISS MANNERS—My son died several years ago. His widow is being married soon. Is it customary for the family of the deceased spouse to be invited to the wedding? They are having a large wedding. If we are not invited, should we send a gift?

GENTLE READER—It is not customary, for fear that the family of the deceased spouse may find such a ceremony painfully reminiscent of the previous wedding. Your question suggests that you are on warm terms with your daughter-in-law and it would be kind of you to let her know that you wish her happiness. This can be done with a letter and, if you wish, a present.

Unmarried Parents

DEAR MISS MANNERS—I never married my daughter's father—he never divorced and I never married. I've seen etiquette rules for divorced parents at their child's wedding, but not for those who were never married.

He still lives with his wife and their grown daughter. He has visited us over the years on a rather regular basis and he has never missed a special occasion. He and my daughter keep in touch and he and I speak occasionally on the phone over family matters. We hold no animosities. At my daughter's wedding my guest will be my "beau" of two years. My daughter's father will be walking her down the aisle, but he will be attending alone. He has never been accepted by most of my family, although he is respected and acknowledged as a true human by my aunt and uncle and by the groom's parents.

What is the proper seating for the church ceremony and the reception? Both men are congenial types, always willing to talk with anyone (and hopefully to each other). We don't want to offend anyone, but most importantly, we do not want to make her father feel unwanted—he is wanted. We also don't want to make my guest feel unnecessary or in the way.

GENTLE READER—Among the things that etiquette is much too polite to pay attention to at a wedding is whether or not the bride's parents were ever married. The marriage that is of interest is the one taking place at the moment, and the relevant characteristic of the parents is that they are her parents.

Normally, the bride's family is grouped together, both at the ceremony and if there is seating at the party afterward. The only reason that ways have recently been found to keep them apart is the fear that they will kill one another. Those parents not currently married are neither required to pretend to be a pair for the occasion nor to keep their distance, unless they and their current partners are not to be trusted together. In your case, you have an amiable set of people, all presumably focused on the bride's happiness, rather than on any previous dissatisfactions of their own. By all means, sit together. Your disgruntled relatives will simply have to accept the harmony among you. Perhaps it will set them an example.

The Birth Mother

DEAR MISS MANNERS—Our daughter gave up a son at birth for adoption. Now, twenty years later, this lad has looked us up and we are delighted. The question is, where do we fit in at his coming wedding? His adopted mother is dead. He has his adopted father, grandmother on one side, and an aunt.

One reason he looked us up is that he was looking for more family. He found his birth mother, two aunts, two cousins and us, a set of grandparents. I don't think it fair to the adoptive father for the birth mother to be in the receiving line. In fact, I wonder if we should be at the wedding at all?

GENTLE READER—As you have sensitively considered, a newly discovered mother does not belong in a line to receive the intimate circle of a family with whom she has not been acquainted. Can you imagine the explanations that would be necessary?

"I'm Jonathan's mother. No, I had nothing to do with his father here. His birth father is—oh, never mind. It was someone else; let's just leave it at that. Of course I know Mrs. Tunis was his mother, although I never actually knew her. But she's dead, you know, and then he went and found me . . ." The receiving line wouldn't budge after the first person started to receive this interesting news. The entire focus of the occasion would be on this relationship, rather than that of the new couple.

This is by no means to say that Miss Manners is opposed to your family's attending the wedding, if the bridegroom's adoptive relatives are not hurt by it. They may even be agreeable to having a minor fuss made over you—say, toasting the newly found relatives at the reception, by way of announcement. But this, as your instinctive courtesy tells you, is not for you to suggest.

Your proposal might be that the lad ask his father how he would feel about any or all of you going to the ceremony only, or attending the reception but merely identifying yourselves as relatives of the bridegroom without going into detail. Even if he welcomes you, it would be well to be careful to show that he is the one with the parental authority (or what can be said to be left of it by the time the child gets married), not your daughter, who turned it over to him.

Respect for Relatives

DEAR MISS MANNERS—On the day before my cousin's wedding, our great-uncle was seriously injured in a car accident. Things were touch and go that night; fortunately, by the morning of the wedding, he was out of danger and his daughter even dropped by the reception to represent that branch of the family and reassure the rest of us that her father would be fine.

Now that I am looking forward to my own wedding, I have begun to wonder what would be proper if a member of the family were to die just a short time before the wedding. (I do hope I don't seem cold-blooded, but I suppose that's the proper way to approach questions of manners—coolly.) Should we cancel the wedding out of respect? I hope not. Go ahead with the ceremony but cut back on the festivities at the reception? Offer a toast in the dead relative's memory and go on with the party? Ignore it altogether?

I'm sure our own emotional reactions would depend on the closeness and affection of the relationship, but I suspect Miss Manners would want to remind us that decisions regarding weddings are not and should not be made solely or even principally to satisfy the feelings of the bride and groom.

GENTLE READER—Miss Manners is pleased to hear that your great-uncle recovered and hopes everyone else is feeling well enough to outlast your wedding. The answer to your question is that the wedding ceremony may still take place if a relative dies, but that a family does not have any sort of a celebration immediately upon the death of one of its members. Unless it is a very distant relation who is stricken, the wedding reception should be canceled.

Miss Manners approves your noting that it is not only the feelings of the bridal couple who are to be considered here. The dead are also to be considered. Respect for the memory of a just-deceased relative is more important than consideration merely of the disappointment friends may feel at the cancellation of a party.

Dissenting Relatives

DEAR MISS MANNERS—My son is getting married in another part of the country. The bride-to-be and her mother are bubbling with excitement over the fancy wedding reception they are staging. They were so determined to hold it at a particular site that the wedding date was delayed by two months.

I don't care for ostentatious wedding-day arrangements. Certainly I will not stand in a receiving line. Nor will I allow my picture to be taken. (I do not like the way I photograph lately; recently, I had my silhouette done, rather than submit to the embarrassment of another picture.) Obviously, I am going to make someone angry if I hold to my principles at the reception. Thus I am thinking of just going to the wedding and not to the party afterward.

Which do you think would be least offensive to the bride and her mother—attending the reception in a way I can tolerate, or just skipping it altogether? If I do attend, I will not make any negative remarks, but neither will I pretend enthusiasm for anything I don't like. My husband, on the other hand, will jovially go through the motions at the reception, and then come home and have a great laugh over his phoniness.

GENTLE READER—Those are interesting principles you have. As Miss Manners understands it, they require sabotaging your son's wedding reception and publicly insulting his bride and her family—out of respect for your sense of style and an odd whim or two.

Miss Manners refuses to recommend either of your solutions. If you are surly at the wedding reception, it will, of course, create a scandal. The inevitable assumption will be that you hate the bride. If you boycott the reception, the assumption will be that it is the bridegroom, your own son, who has done something so appalling that you cannot forgive him.

In neither case could you expect to have much of a relationship with the couple after the wedding. The wound you so righteously talk of inflicting will be a serious one. Miss Manners suggests you adopt your husband's solution. The parents of bridegrooms often laugh as they congratulate themselves on how superior their taste is to the other family's. But the principled ones do this strictly in private.

10

THE ATTENDANTS

Chief Duties of the Maid or Matron of Honor

1. Continues to act as the bride's best friend to the extent of listening to confidences and helping with tasks even when driven to distraction by the repetition of petty worries and details.
2. Attends all wedding-related functions and becomes spontaneously moved to gather bridesmaids and other intimates of the bride for a shower.
3. Fusses over the bride on the day of the wedding, helping her dress, telling her that her doubts about the bridegroom are only traditional bridal jitters, taking charge of the bride's bouquet during the ceremony, gracefully straightening her train, and producing the bridegroom's ring at the appropriate moment.

Chief Duties of the Best Man

1. Delivers the bridegroom to the ceremony at the proper time, correctly dressed, and in a

suitable frame of mind—which is induced by (a.) sending him home early the night before and (b.) reminding him that he adores the bride and is not making a mistake.

2. Supervises the ushers, checking out their clothing, encouraging them to ask the bridesmaids, and especially the junior bridesmaids, to dance, and vetoing any ideas for jokes that would shock guests or disable the going-away vehicle.

3. Offers a flattering toast to the bride, omitting any details about the courtship or the bridegroom's character that the bride's grandparents might not want to know.

4. Produces the bride's ring during the ceremony, either from his pocket or by nudging the ring-bearer, and the tickets for the wedding trip at the conclusion of the reception.

Chief Duties of the Bridesmaids

1. Be good sports about the bride's taste in their dresses, jollying her into a compromise that they can both stomach and afford, and then putting up with the results.

2. Keep smiling charmingly, not only while marching up the aisle together, but while marching back down it on the arms of ushers they may not fancy, while standing in the receiving line, and while going around the reception accepting silly compliments.

Chief Duties of the Ushers

1. Keep their right arms bent before the ceremony to seat the lady wedding guests, while

the gentlemen follow behind; and again at the ceremony's conclusion, to escort the brides- maids down the aisle.

2. Be good sports about restraining their sense of fun on the grounds that the occasion may seem a complete joke to them, but apparently has a serious element for their friend the bridegroom.

Bridesmaid Abuse

"Would you be so kind as to abolish the institution of bridesmaid?"

Miss Manners was startled at the request, but only for a moment. It was no accident that it came from a meticu- lously polite young lady who also happens to have lots of friends and looks wonderful in pastel dresses, even ones with bows on the backside.

Bridesmaid abuse has become rampant, and it isn't the groomsmen who are inflicting it. At least such is not the thrust of the complaints addressed to Miss Manners. The outrages she hears about result either from tyranny on the part of the bride, or from the observance of an unwieldy accumulation of unauthorized but persistent cus- toms that have made what ought to be a pleasurable duty of friendship into a social and financial burden.

Before absolutely abolishing the post of bridesmaid, Miss Manners will attempt to return some perspective to it and to restore humane working conditions. If this doesn't work, she will find herself in support of those who resolve to decline politely any such honors that may be proposed to them.

The original point of having bridesmaids was that the bride would wish, at this momentous occasion in her life, to be surrounded by her closest friends. That a group of young ladies might add a decorative element to the ceremony, and that they might want to fuss over the bride a bit because their fondness for her filled them with vicarious happiness, were merely delightful but incidental advantages.

These two factors have now come to overwhelm the intention of the institution. Things have come to the point where bridesmaids' appearance is as strictly mandated and inspected as if they were in boot camp and their kindnesses are no more optional than if they had been conscripted.

The attributes of prettiness and willingness to perform extra services may be considered so important by the bride that the mere fact that someone has been her lifelong friend may no longer be enough to qualify her for bridesmaidhood. Miss Manners is always hearing of cases where the bride wants to eliminate from her entourage a friend who doesn't have the right look, or doesn't make herself available for chores, in favor of a comparative stranger who looks the part or is willing to enter service.

Thus the institution of bridesmaidhood may abolish itself without Miss Manners's intervention. The time cannot be far away when some entrepreneur puts forth the advantages of hiring professionals for the occasion, rather than having to depend on mere friends.

The fact is that the only real duty of a bridesmaid is to hang around the altar during the ceremony, paying attention and looking pleased or moved (both, if she can manage it without getting so carried away that she stands on the bride's train). Being chief bridesmaid, known as maid or matron of honor, does carry light duties in addition to witnessing the ceremony—holding the bride's bouquet as she receives her wedding ring, producing the bridegroom's wedding ring when it is needed, and keeping an eye out in case the bridal finery needs straightening or the bride's new mother-in-law has left lipstick on her cheek.

That's it. Contrary to rumor, bridesmaids are not obliged to entertain in honor of the bride, nor to wear clothes that they cannot afford and that make them look stupid. Because bridesmaids are supposed to be such good friends of the bride, they often do get together to give a shower or a luncheon in her honor. It is charming, and even usual, for them to be so moved, but it is not obligatory. From the same wish to please their friend, the bridesmaids should listen tolerantly to her ideas of what dresses might be pretty on them for the occasion. Personally, Miss Manners prefers to see bridesmaids dressed similarly rather than identically, but the specifics of either should be arrived at by a consensus among those most concerned.

What a bride needs in order to ensure their cooperation with her plans is exactly what ought to form her basis for asking these ladies to honor her with their presence: affection. If she spent her energies cultivating that, rather than issuing orders, she would be more successful, not to mention more bridal.

The "Best Person"

DEAR MISS MANNERS—I am to be involved in a wedding in which two of my dearest friends will marry each other. In lieu of a best man, the groom has asked me, a female, to act as "best person." This is an honor and I am touched as well as proud of my friend's openmindedness.

It has come to my attention that some of the other women in the bridal party are apprehensive in regard to my role in the wedding, a formal church ceremony. I wish to be sensitive to the feelings of those who may be uncomfortable with this break with tradition, as well as being correct in my behavior.

GENTLE READER—It troubles Miss Manners to think what those bridesmaids might be apprehensive about. Do they imagine that one of them will have to dance with you at the reception? Do they think of the recessional as a parade of pseudo-romantic couples?

All this would be silly. Traditionally, the bridegroom is attended by his best friend, friendship being the chief factor, not gender. Of course you will dress as a lady and dance with gentlemen. You will not offer any lady your arm, but merely march at the maid of honor's side as paired bridesmaids do in a processional. But if the bride's honor attendant is a gentleman, he may offer you his arm.

Mother as Matron of Honor

DEAR MISS MANNERS—I have asked my mother to be my matron of honor. I have no close female friends and my mother and I have a close relationship. Despite these facts, she fears that it would be incorrect. She promised to abide by your advice.

GENTLE READER—Miss Manners wishes her great happiness in the role. How odd it is that there has long been the custom of bridegrooms selecting their fathers for the best-friend role of "best man," but not for brides' selecting their mothers.

Sister

DEAR MISS MANNERS—I am considering getting married again. The time before, my sister was my matron of honor. I would dearly love her to fill that role again, but in discussing it, we thought that this might be frowned on or socially unacceptable.

GENTLE READER—What, pray, is your reasoning? That when changing husbands, it looks backward to retain the same sister?

Pregnant Bridesmaid

DEAR MISS MANNERS—My granddaughter is being married and among her bridesmaids will be a lady who will be nine months pregnant, walking along with the other bridesmaids. My opinion is that she would be out of place among them. Would it be in good taste? I am eighty-three years old, and my children believe I'm old-fashioned.

GENTLE READER—Indeed, pregnancy was once considered to be in poor taste and signs of it best concealed. This was a tremendous inconvenience to ladies who got pregnant anyway and is a fashion that Miss Manners is delighted to see gone.

Presuming there is no question of physical difficulty for the lady in question, she should properly take her place as a bridesmaid by virtue of being one of the bride's friends. Her own family situation is irrelevant to the occasion.

Widow

DEAR MISS MANNERS—I am a widow and my friend has asked me to be her honor attendant in her wedding. Would I be called the matron or maid of honor?

GENTLE READER—Miss Manners does not want to be the one to break the news to you that maidenhood is not renewable. So she will confine herself to saying that a widow would have to be a matron of honor.

Ring Bearers and Flower Girls

DEAR MISS MANNERS—My fiancé and I are trying to finalize the members of the wedding party. Should the ring bearer and the flower girl be a certain age, or is it up to each couple to decide?

GENTLE READER—The ring bearer and the flower girl are supposed to be of an age to make everyone smile and nudge one another and say "Awwwww, looooooook" during the processional. A mere "Don't they look cute?" with no extra letters in the pronunciation means that the young people are old enough to be a junior bridesmaid and usher. What age produces the desired effect is something that the bridal couple may decide.

Whatever their ages, Miss Manners urges you to fuss a bit over the younger members of your bridal party. Children in weddings usually treat their roles with great seriousness and share the bridal couple's sense of the importance of the occasion. They also frequently retain vivid memories of such events, which they trot out a decade or two later when they want "a wedding just like Cousin Adelaide's."

A Mother's Wedding

DEAR MISS MANNERS—My twenty-eight-year-old daughter will be marrying for the second time and she would like her seven-year-old daughter to be a flower girl. But she feels that her eight-year-old son is a little old to be a ring bearer, and would like him to come in from the side, as is the custom in our church, with the groom and groomsmen, and stand next to the best man at the altar. Do you agree that he is too old to be a ring bearer, and if so, is this a viable alternative? In either case, what would be the proper attire? Neither of us cares for tuxes on little boys, but we feel he is too big for short pants.

GENTLE READER—Miss Manners finds herself amused at how you managed, with one question, to arouse both what is rigid about etiquette and what is flexible. She is in the peculiar position of wanting to back you up and to lighten you up at the same time.

Absolutely, miniature versions of gentlemen's evening clothes should not be worn by boys under the age of eighteen. Miss Manners is even more firm about that than you are. But she would never, never try to explain to a child that the one-year age difference between him and his sister means that she will have a role in the wedding party and he will not. No rule of etiquette draws such a fine line, which is likely to arouse such hurt feelings. It is to deal with precisely this kind of problem that the positions of junior groomsman and junior bridesmaid were created.

However, in this case, Miss Manners would prefer to have both children standing at the altar witnessing the ceremony at close hand, since it affects them so directly. She is not, frankly, enamored of the idea of having one's children as bridal attendants. But given the choice, she would choose an inclusive arrangement over an exclusive one any time.

Bridesmaid's Tattoo

DEAR MISS MANNERS—I am to be a bridesmaid and the bride let us pick out our own dresses, as long as they were velvet and not strapless. Wheee, I found this elegant off-the-shoulder dress.

I have a tattoo on my right shoulder that shows. I don't know if I should cover it with special makeup (the bride's sister thinks I should) or leave it alone. The tattoo is now a part of me and they should accept me the way I am. I am a middle-class woman, well groomed, clean, not the biker type.

The bride really doesn't care if I cover it or not, but I feel as if she's not telling me her real feelings about the matter from not wanting to hurt my feelings. She's a really good friend. I feel if everyone at this wedding is so offended by my tattoo and not more interested in the wedding day, then they have a problem.

GENTLE READER—Okay, what's the tattoo look like?

Never mind. Unless it is positively nauseating or obscene, Miss Manners is going to surprise you by defending it. Wheee! (as you would say).

It is silly enough that bridesmaids are required to wear the same dress, without their subjecting their bodies or hair to criticism. The notion that the bride can make them restyle their hair or change their weight in the hopes of standardizing them into a matching set is as insulting as it is silly. This bride has done nothing of the kind. She has been faultlessly polite—and yet you are goading her to tell you her true feelings. Miss Manners feels that if you are not more interested in your friend's wedding than in her opinion of your tattoo, it is you who have a problem.

Never, Ever Black

DEAR MISS MANNERS—Our sister is having an evening July wedding at which the five girls in our family, all over the age of twenty-eight, will be attendants. We are all on a limited budget and would like to purchase a dress we could wear again. We have suggested black, but the groom's mother feels black is inappropriate. I have read that it is acceptable for bridesmaids to wear black in an evening wedding.

GENTLE READER—Not here, you didn't. Miss Manners has never understood, much less espoused, the Oh-Well-Who-Really-Cares? School of Etiquette.

That is not to say that customs do not sometimes change and that etiquette should not embrace changes that are for the good. But that a keeper of manners should succumb to thoughtless change, just because it is tiring to try to point out the difference between good change and bad, strikes her as outrageous.

Black is the traditional color of mourning, and confusing the symbolism of marriage and death is a particularly unfortunate idea. While formal mourning has gone out of practice (a change with both good and bad aspects, but we'll leave that argument for another time), the symbolism remains for many people, including, in this case, the bridegroom's very own mother. To these people, the wedding would not look chic but sad.

Negotiating

DEAR MISS MANNERS—Although I was honored when I was asked to be a bridesmaid, I am having second thoughts. We had already been fitted for gowns and I had paid for a fitting. Now the couple wants to suit the entire bridal party in tuxedos! I won't wear a tuxedo. I think it's silly. My fiancé is to be best man and I don't wish to look like his brother. Should I decline and hurt my friend's feelings? What should I say?

GENTLE READER—My, what fun everyone will have trying to tell the sheep from the goats. And won't the bride look adorable? Friendship may require fulfilling a lot of difficult but legitimate demands, but making a fool of oneself in public is not one of them.

Miss Manners doesn't usually recommend that bridal attendants organize job actions and set non-negotiable working conditions, but desperate measures are called for. She suggests that you, as a friend of the bride, and your fiancé, as the bridegroom's best friend, have a serious talk with these people. If they do not listen to reason, bring in the other bridesmaids. Miss Manners is confident that they will be willing to help bring these people to their senses—if not for reasons of taste, perhaps because they have already made an investment in other clothes.

"Take this job and . . ."

DEAR MISS MANNERS—A friend I used to work with asked me to be in her wedding party a year later. Reluctantly, I gave in and said okay.

All this time, there has been no talk of wedding plans or any kind of get-together among the attendants, who don't know one another. This friend and I are not as chummy as we were five years ago; in fact, I spoke to her only a handful of times since she called me. I've had two very, very last-minute invitations to her apartment for some kind of parties. (I thought it was inconsiderate of her to call me at 7:30 and expect me and my date to be over at her place by 8, so I never promised I'd be there and went about what I had planned in the first place.)

When I call her I get:

1. The answering machine, and my message is never returned.
2. "I've got company" or "Can I talk to you later?" and she never calls back.
3. The Call Waiting modality where she puts our conversation on hold, and when we are disconnected, she never even calls back to say "sorry" or "good-bye."

I'm totally baffled by her actions and the whole situation. At this point, I can't continue to plan around some wedding I'm supposed to be in, while screwing up my life, my vacation plans and possibly my own wedding. My mom is on my case to call the bride-to-be and find out the details of the wedding. I say no—let her call me to say what's going on. After all, she asked me to be in her wedding.

What is the proper way to get some information without putting her on the spot? I'm beginning to believe she forgot she asked me to be in her wedding, or she changed her mind and thought she told me but really didn't. I'd like to tell her I've changed my mind, or something suddenly came up. Is it right for me to do that?

GENTLE READER—Miss Manners joins your mother to the extent of insisting that you get this cleared up before you make other plans, and of believing that you must take the initiative, as the bride has lamentably failed to do so.

You make a convincing case that the friendship is no longer one in which it would be appropriate for you to be her bridesmaid. If the wedding were imminent, you would have to go ahead with it to avoid disrupting her plans. A year-old invitation to a far-distant wedding, without the reinforcement of continued discussion, is not that binding.

Just avoid blaming her or offering trivial excuses. To say that you find you are going to be married at about the same time is a legitimate excuse, if true, but to seem to value a vacation above something as important as a wedding is offensive. Write her a letter saying how honored you were to have been chosen, how sorry you are that you find you cannot be in her wedding after all, and how much happiness you wish her.

11

THE WEDDING GUESTS

Chief Duties of the Wedding Guests

1. Answer the invitation immediately and definitely, in the style (third person or informal letter) in which it was written, and only on behalf of those to whom it was addressed—and then fulfill the pledge to show up (having made their own travel arrangements) or (even if that better offer fell through) not to show up.
2. Be moved to send (but never bring) wedding presents, bearing in mind that it is nice, but not strictly necessary, to give a second wedding present for the same person's second marriage, nor more than a note of congratulation to an acquaintance whose wedding they do not care to attend; and also bearing in mind that while it is desirable to please the couple, it is not necessary to comply with any rude attempts to direct what the guests are to buy, donate, or contribute.
3. Dress according to the formality of the occasion (neither in white nor, except for gentlemen's evening clothes, black), rather than

defy it in the name of comfort or personal style.

4. Head for the receiving line immediately upon arriving at the reception (telling the bride's and bridegroom's mothers and any fathers present that it was a beautiful wedding; the bride, that she is beautiful and that they wish her the best; the bridegroom, that they congratulate him and that he is a lucky man; and the bridesmaids, that they look beautiful), after which they may get a drink and socialize with other guests, provided they do not use the occasion to inquire into these people's prospects of being married.

Accepting a Wedding Invitation

DEAR MISS MANNERS—Back in the olden days, one replied to a wedding invitation by writing an abbreviated copy of it, starting with one's own name:

> *Mr. and Mrs. John Jones*
> *accept with pleasure*
> *the kind invitation of*
> *Mr. and Mrs. Roberts*
> *for Saturday, the tenth of June*
> *at half after seven o'clock*
> *City Club*

Is this form of reply passé? What is currently the proper method of replying?

GENTLE READER—Passé in what sense? There is no need to update this form, as it is succinct and correct. It is not for guests to treat the style of the occasion with less formality than the hosts do.

Miss Manners does not deny that an awful lot of people have declared the necessity of answering invitations at all to be out of fashion. Since they are not the hosts, they have kindly taken it upon themselves to declare that hosts "don't care any more" to know who is attending their events.

This is a shameless falsehood. Ask anyone connected with giving a wedding. The timid will declare that they themselves don't care, but that the caterer does, which isn't true, either—they do care, and the caterer is satisfied if all the meals ordered are paid for, whether or not they are eaten. Therefore, the olden days, as you call them, are still upon us and will be forever, or at least until such time as people get fed up entertaining ingrates and stop issuing invitations.

Declining a Wedding Invitation

DEAR MISS MANNERS—Here is my plight: I am a single, middle-aged man with no intent of marriage. I have celebrated many weddings of friends, relatives and colleagues, as either guest or groomsman. Now I'm receiving invitations to the many more weddings for the children of these couples. Though they have my best wishes, I have no desire to participate either with my attendance or by providing gifts. How may I politely express my position?

GENTLE READER—You are in luck. Etiquette has taken the precaution of supplying the exact words you need; you have only to fill in your name at the top, neatly centered. It is:

Mr. Algernon Asquith
regrets exceedingly that he is unable to accept
the very kind invitation of
Mr. and Mrs. Quiverful
for Saturday, the eleventh of June

Miss Manners only asks that you do not fool with this wording, in the disastrous hope of personalizing it to your situation. There is no polite way to say that a gentleman thinks he has gone quite far enough in enduring the nuptial festivities of his friends without boring himself senseless at those of their children.

Response Cards

DEAR MISS MANNERS—In a wedding invitation from a very influential family, I looked for a response card, but there was none. On the invitation itself, on the lower left-hand corner, were the initials "R.s.v.p." with no date to return a response by.

Since I thought this was odd, I asked my sister, who replied that this is now the proper way and that we were supposed to buy our own response cards to send back. I disagree and think the party involved should send response cards. Who is right?

GENTLE READER—Has it come to this? That people who refrain from doing something incorrect are now being thought rude by the very people who violate the rule themselves? Allow Miss Manners a minute to sit down and search for her vinaigrette.

She suggests that you also take a minute to think. What you are saying is that people who offer you hospitality must also be responsible for seeing to it that you answer their invitation. Response cards were never correct. They are a desperate, and not particularly successful, way to make up for the extreme rudeness of people who think it too much trouble to inform their hosts whether or not they will attend an occasion to which they have been kindly bidden. Wedding invitations are properly answered on your very own paper, with your very own hand. Following the form of the invitation, they say either that "Mr. and Mrs. Phiffle accept with pleasure" or "regret exceedingly that they are unable to accept" the kind invitation of their hosts.

Using Response Cards Anyway

DEAR MISS MANNERS—How can one decline an invitation including an engraved response card that has a blank space indicating the number of guests attending? Placing a zero on the blank with no explanation seems ridiculous.

GENTLE READER—Writing a zero on the card provided is, Miss Manners agrees, unspeakable. But you could put a dash there, and write a brief statement of regret ("So sorry I can't be there—very best wishes") after it.

Consequences

DEAR MISS MANNERS—My husband and I spent our own money to treat ourselves and others with a grand celebration of our decision to marry. We spent six months of our life, and thousands of dollars, planning a big wedding. Many families we invited R.s.v.p.'d for the entire family, or for the husband and wife. Unfortunately, we discovered that many husbands and children "do not like to go to weddings." Out of the 150 guests expected at the wedding, only 40 showed up.

Miss Manners, I do not care about the money we wasted. What hurt was the emotional devastation we felt when we stood to walk down the aisle of a church filled with loved ones, and discovered that the church was empty, save for two rows. It was the same feeling when we entered a large reception hall with place settings for 150 people, and found only 30 people. This was supposed to be our wedding day, one of the best days of our life, and it was horrible. I wanted to write this letter to let people know what happens when they decide not to go to a wedding, or think that sending one representative of the family is sufficient to satisfy any social obligations they may feel.

GENTLE READER—Miss Manners knew this is where we would end up once people started regarding social invitations as negotiable, transferable, and nonbinding. Going to the pseudo-parties given by businesses and patronizing restaurants has given people the incredibly rude idea that among their friends, as well, they may send representatives, drop by or not as their moods dictate, bring extra people, demand special foods and so on.

Wedding invitations are particularly sacred, but all social invitations must be treated with respect or there will be no order, pleasure, or point in extending hospitality. Miss Manners hopes people will learn from your experience and is sorry you had to be the victim of such callousness. But please don't remember this as just a horrible day. You had each other, didn't you?

Conflicting Events

DEAR MISS MANNERS—The planned dates of my high school reunion and my brother-in-law's wedding are the same. Do I have to attend the wedding?

GENTLE READER—Yes. Only if your brother-in-law starts getting married every five years, in synchronization with your reunions, will Miss Manners allow you to consider neglecting such a major family occasion in favor of an alumni event.

Not Bills

DEAR MISS MANNERS—You have not mentioned the fact that a wedding invitation is really a wedding announcement. So many people have decidedly fluttery guilt feelings about being invited to weddings of people they really don't know. Is it proper to send these newlyweds a card wishing them happiness? Isn't a person obliged to send a gift when invited to the reception? If this were not the case, wouldn't you have to send a gift to every couple whose announcement is printed in the newspaper?

GENTLE READER—Miss Manners begs your pardon, but kindly requests you not to add to the confusion. A wedding invitation is a wedding invitation, not a wedding announcement. A wedding announcement is a wedding announcement. The former asks you in advance to attend a wedding, and the latter informs you afterward that one has taken place.

Your problem is that you think that one or both of them is actually a bill. Why do so many people have trouble believing that there is no way at all that bridal couples, or anyone else, can send a social communication that informs people that they must ante up? It is true that when the matter is voluntary, nice people are supposed to want to give their marrying friends some tangible evidence of their delight. Thus attending a wedding is associated with the giving of a present.

If one doesn't actually much care about the marriage, one need only decline the invitation and send good wishes to the couple. Wishes for happiness are the proper response to a wedding announcement, although those, too, occasionally inspire people to send presents.

Not Theater Tickets

DEAR MISS MANNERS—A girlfriend of mine and her husband were invited to a wedding. Her husband cannot attend, due to a prior commitment. My friend has asked me to attend with her. The bride is an acquaintance of mine, but more friendly with my girlfriend. Because I was not formally invited to the wedding by the bride, but will attend as a guest of my friend, am I required to give a separate wedding gift?

GENTLE READER—No, you are not required to send a wedding present because you are not going to attend the wedding. Miss Manners will go so far as to say that you are required not to attend the wedding.

A wedding invitation addressed to a married couple is not like a pair of theater tickets that may be transferred to others. It is not fair to bridal couples to populate their weddings with guests-once-removed—people to whom they are not close but who are the guests of their guests. Had the bride wished to invite you to the wedding, she would have done so.

Not a Referendum

DEAR MISS MANNERS—We are a couple in our sixties. The twenty-eight-year-old daughter of good friends of ours has invited us to a commitment ceremony for herself and her female lover. They lived together for several years and now are throwing a big bash, with vows, many guests, and a reception.

We do not approve of this lifestyle, but of course would not make a big show of refusing the invitation. We are wondering, however, if we can refuse and, if so, if we should say why, or if we should invent a prior engagement. There really seems to be no happy solution. We don't want to lie and we don't want to butt in with our opinion of homosexuality, nor do we want to attend an event that would make us uncomfortable.

GENTLE READER—An invitation is not a referendum, in which guests are asked to give their opinions of the arrangement being celebrated. It is a mere inquiry as to whether you would like to be present, and in this case, the answer is no.

Miss Manners assures you that you do not need to lie in order to avoid explaining your objections. You need merely decline politely. Although no specific excuse is necessary, it is customary to accompany this with a congratulatory wish, which Miss Manners trusts you can supply in good conscience. Wishing someone happiness does not involve you in debating how happiness is best achieved.

Invitations to Cater

DEAR MISS MANNERS—This wedding invitation enclosure card ("Miss Manners says it's okay if you would like to help with donations of food for the reception") left me and other recipients speechless. Since you never seem at a loss for words, would you please comment.

GENTLE READER—Miss Manners is speechless, too, and you will have to excuse her, because when she recovers, the first person she wants to talk to will be her lawyer. Not only did Miss Manners never say any such thing, but she is on record as being violently opposed to the notion of issuing nonhospitable invitations.

Guests (as opposed to those who may volunteer to help, or who respond to a suggestion that everyone pitch in on a cooperative event with no particular host) are not expected to bring their own hospitality along with them. "We're getting married and we expect you to cater the reception" is not an acceptable way to entertain.

Volunteering

DEAR MISS MANNERS—My first cousin is getting married, and his mother, my aunt, keeps saying, "It is going to be a small wedding." By that, I assume she is saying I won't be invited. I don't care about myself, but my youngest daughter, who is ten, has never been to a wedding in her life. My oldest daughter, eighteen, has not been to one since she was five. I want very much for them both to at least observe the wedding ceremony. I would be willing for them to pass on the reception, etc. I am on excellent terms with my aunt, but how do I approach her on this subject? I heard that a church is a public place, so a wedding can be observed by anybody. True?

GENTLE READER—Technically, you are right. But Miss Manners promises you that should you take advantage of this, you will no longer be on excellent terms with your aunt. Any way you or your daughter attempt to attend this wedding to which you are not invited—by making any kind of a plea, or by simply dropping by—will be interpreted as a reproach for their not having invited you. And it will create a major embarrassment for your relatives who expect to go off to whatever small celebration they are having, without you.

By the way, Miss Manners, susceptible as she is to maternal solicitude, has failed to be touched by your argument in favor of your daughters. A wedding is not a show to be viewed simply for the experience or amusement.

Parental Discretion

DEAR MISS MANNERS—I have received an invitation to my cousin's wedding, addressed to my husband, myself, and our four children, ages nine and a half to one and a half. My aunt, the mother of the bride, told my father that she was upset when she heard I was thinking of hiring a babysitter, at least for the two youngest, because she desired all my children to attend. She loves children, especially tots, no matter how rambunctious they are. I know she wouldn't bat an eye if a youngster ran up the aisle or cried through the service. On the whole, my children are sweet and well behaved, and many enjoy their company. However, most times they are typical children and behave as such.

I'm afraid the scene might be this: The four-year-old will talk loudly through the whole service, the two-year-old will flirt with the people behind him, and the one-year-old will want to get down and go off to observe on his own. My husband will not be able to attend and help me. Although my dad would lean over backward to assist me, I don't want to put him in the position of parenting my children at an affair at which he should be enjoying himself. And quite frankly, if I had to spend time in the back of the church, outside, or running after them during the reception, I'd just as soon stay home.

Miss Manners, I want to honor my aunt's wishes. I know she will be disappointed if I only bring part of my brood, but the thought of less than a perfect day exhausts me.

GENTLE READER—You have no idea how refreshing Miss Manners found your letter. To understand that, you would have to see the piles of correspondence she has from people who are vehemently opposed to having any children at family occasions, and from their relatives who are equally vehement about bringing theirs, whether it is appropriate or not.

How nice of your aunt to take such a warm interest in your children, above the technical perfection of the occasion. And how nice of you to take such a warm interest in the occasion, above the natural limitations of your children to tolerate. While hosts are within the bounds of politeness to invite adults-only to a wedding, the parent of invited children is the one to make the decision. (Miss Manners's awkward wording is to head off any misinterpretation that a parent can make the decision about the attendance of children who were not invited.)

You make a strong case for not bringing yours. The polite way to say so, given the hospitality of your aunt, is "You are so sweet to include them, but, really, they're not old enough to appreciate and enjoy it. They'll be happier hearing about it, and meeting the couple on an occasion when they can really enjoy their attention."

Discretion

DEAR MISS MANNERS—The man with whom I have had an "affair" for the last fifteen years is getting married. Technically, I guess it hasn't been an affair, since neither of us was married or in significant monogamous relationships. However, the sexual aspects of our relationship were quite important and were hidden from our various other friends.

He plans to invite me to the wedding. After all, I am one of his closer and longer friends and to not invite me would raise suspicions, he says. Should I go? I will, of course, send a present. Any particular presents that should be avoided or that you would recommend? We have stopped our sexual encounters; however, he continues to visit me occasionally alone, as well as sometimes with his fiancée. Would it be proper for us (or him) to let her know our history?

GENTLE READER—Let us take that last question first; Miss Manners has the feeling it is the key to the rest. What, pray, did you have in mind? A luncheon with the lady during which you wait until she has a mouthful of chef's salad before murmuring, "I don't know if Jeremy happened to mention this to you, but . . ."? Warning the gentleman that the next time they pay one of their visits, you expect him to sit with you on the sofa, facing her, and to say, after simultaneously clearing your throats, "By the way, there is something we think you should know"?

Surely the gentleman's history is his to confide or not, as he sees fit, and in a manner of his own choosing. To suggest otherwise is something very close to blackmail. You would not care to have him coming around in the future, should you form a serious attachment, with an offer to enlighten the gentleman.

Your quibble about what does or does not constitute an affair suggests that you believe that the only legitimate hurt one can inflict is deception, and you seem to count not confessing the past as deception In his remark about not arousing suspicion, the gentleman has indicated that he disagrees.

The answer to your questions about attending his wedding and choosing a present is to continue the discretion you showed, when it was presumably in your own interest, now that it is no longer your concern. As the visits seem to have worked, Miss Manners presumes you are enough under control of your behavior to attend the wedding under the guise of innocent friendship. Your present, also, should be in keeping with that relationship. A photograph album of your last trip with him would, for example, be in bad taste.

Skipping the Ceremony on Principle

DEAR MISS MANNERS—When my wife and I get invited to the wedding of a son or daughter of our friends, we usually don't go to the church part, but always go to the wedding reception. We make sure to talk to the bride and groom and always bring a gift.

The reason that we don't go to the church is because I'm not a religious person and my wife is not a member of a major religion and this is known to our friends. But a number of people not involved in the weddings have let their displeasure be known to us in no uncertain terms. Are we obligated to go to the church if we want to exercise our desire to go to the reception? Are we inconsiderate and does this give them the right to be rude to us?

GENTLE READER—Miss Manners does not recall "the right to be rude" as being in the Bill of Rights and grants it to no one. But she can certainly see how you and your wife tempted these people beyond endurance. Attending a wedding ceremony is not an expression of one's own religion, or an endorsement of anyone else's. It is participation in a ceremonial milestone in the lives of people who are important to you, in a way that merely attending their social events is not. What you and your wife have done, by following your idiosyncratic reasoning unrelated to the understanding and customs of the society, is to establish the idea that you attend parties but not more serious events.

Entertainment

DEAR MISS MANNERS—Living in Miami, we are surrounded by both Spanish and English. Recently, my husband and I were invited to a wedding and the entire hour-and-a-half ceremony was in Spanish. Unfortunately, I am not fluent in Spanish, and my attention span did not last ninety minutes. Should a couple inform the guests on the invitation if a wedding is to be in Spanish, so each can choose whether or not to attend?

GENTLE READER—You certainly have a peculiar way of choosing whether to attend a wedding. It is Miss Manners's understanding that wedding guests are there out of affection for the bridal couple, not in the expectation of riveting entertainment adjusted to whatever their attention spans happen to be. Unfortunately, there is no way to indicate on a wedding invitation that unsuitable people should decline. If there were, it would read "If you don't care about us, don't bother to attend."

The Obligations of "And Guest"

DEAR MISS MANNERS—I am a divorced woman. When I am invited to a wedding, birthday, or any other special occasion, it is addressed to me "and guest." Is it customary for the guest to pay some of the expenses, such as for his dinner or for the gift? I assume that since he is my guest, I do not expect him to pay for anything. However, what if he asks or wants to contribute? In the card, if I am paying for the monetary gift that is enclosed, do I sign my name only, or do I write his name too, although he made no contribution? Does he also write in the guest book? Since I am inviting him to go to the party with me, is it customary for me to pick him up, since I'm going there anyway?

GENTLE READER—You are asking for rules on a practice that Miss Manners considers wrong. Inquiring of one's friends "Who is that charming man you've been seeing?" so as to invite him by name is one thing; giving one's guests two slots each, the other to be filled however that person wishes, is another. The result is that occasions that should be celebrated by one's intimates are half populated by strangers.

Now that Miss Manners has gotten that off her chest, she will address the reality of the situation. Yes, the gentleman is your guest and should not be asked to pay anything, or to buy a present for a stranger. (Who drives whom is a matter of convenience.) However, as he did attend, his name should appear with yours in the guest book. That at least gives his hosts a chance to find out afterward who was there.

Fielding Questions

DEAR MISS MANNERS—I have just received the joyous news that my younger brother is to be married in a little over a year. While I share his excitement, I am already dreading the wedding day for one reason: I am gay.

In and of itself, this should not cause such strong anxiety. However, I anticipate that many of my more distant relatives will attend who are unaware of my sexual orientation. I also expect them to start asking me (and my immediate family) questions about my plans for marriage, as I am nine years older than my brother. Obviously, I have no such plans.

Because I am open about my sexual preference, at almost any other social function I would probably just tell them the truth and add that I have been living happily with a wonderful man for several years, dismissing any distress at that response as the querist's problem. At my brother's wedding, however, I feel that such honesty would detract attention from my brother's special day and place it unwillingly on me. This was an issue at my sister's wedding several years ago.

I don't want to offend my relatives, as such questions are neither prying nor insensitive and are politely meant to engage me in friendly conversation. Yet I would like to discourage such conversation from the beginning. To complicate matters, I expect that my lover will also be invited to the wedding, as my other immediate family members welcome him as a member of our family.

GENTLE READER—Miss Manners appreciates your delicacy in not wanting to make your brother's wedding into a coming-out party for yourself. She also would like to note that "When are you going to get married?" is about the most unpleasant conversation opener there is, for anyone of whom it might be asked, at a wedding or anywhere else. But she notices that the wedding is a year off. Surely your family will have some opportunity to be in touch, informally, during that time, with the relatives who will be attending. They could easily slip in a pre-introduction to your lover, and mention how happy they are to have him in the family. Although Miss Manners does not believe in announcing anything about one's sex life, including its orientation, your living arrangement is properly of interest to those who care about you.

12

THE
PRESENTS

W e've been living together for ages, so we have already everything we need."

"We've both been married before, so we have two of everything."

Are those the statements of people who would truly rather not receive any presents?

Oh, perhaps. Every once in a while, Miss Manners actually does hear from someone who is genuinely embarrassed at the idea that inviting intimates to a celebration generally brings forth tangible offerings.

More often, she hears these remarks from people who not only don't object to receiving presents, but are way ahead of the potential givers in thoughts about how best to please the recipients—themselves. If they can't actually surprise themselves, they at least want to do everything else connected with giving the presents they will receive—except, of course, paying for them.

How, they inquire, can they ask guests to get together and sponsor, for example, a major holiday trip? Or how, they ask with even greater candor, can they just get guests to donate cash? Such a useful present and easy to wrap.

If you will allow Miss Manners to mix in some ranting about the vulgarity of this approach, she promises to help make presents do what they are supposed to do, which is to please. The fact is that much of present-giving has become a burden in both directions, which is one reason (the other reasons being greed on the one hand and laziness on the other) that it has deteriorated into the mechanical transfer of money or selection of an item from the recipient's shopping list.

Miss Manners acknowledges that there are many for whom the traditional household presents are not appropriate. She is not as unsympathetic as she pretends with the exasperation of those who deplore the waste of money on unwanted goods. But first we must change attitudes; then we can see about changing the goods.

It is necessary for the preservation of civility to maintain the idea that generosity is—well, generosity. You are not supposed to seem to count on receiving presents—and as a matter of fact, presents for second weddings are not particularly traditional. Nor are presents supposed to be compensation to the celebrants for their expenditure on food and drink. It should also be remembered that guests are guests. Should they happen to be moved to give something they think might be enjoyed, there should be a pretense that they have been successful. You have to seem pleased and grateful.

Attempting to crush out of these well-wishers any impulse to exercise their own thoughts or taste is a mistake. (For that matter, Miss Manners won't even let the nice people put "No gifts," or that painful pun about wanting the guests' "presence, not presents," on their invitations.) Rather, their thoughtfulness should be encouraged.

People who claim to have "everything" have not, it seems, done all the shopping they plan to do for the rest of their lives. They merely mean that they have the staples that once characterized wedding presents. If this isn't obvious to their friends, they may—but only if asked—say modestly, "Oh, we really have all the basic household things," leaving unsaid but obvious the idea that little luxuries would be appreciated.

If the guest cares about the people concerned, he or she should be willing to undertake the obligation to try to think of what would be suitable and pleasing. (Those who don't care enough should decline the invitation and be done with it.) Occasionally people are bound to guess wrong, which is why it is a good idea to make the place of purchase obvious and not inquire after items that may have been discreetly exchanged.

A household where there is enough flatware and appliances can usually use an extra picture frame or vase; most people welcome a case of champagne; many people are known to have an appetite for art books or compact discs. Miss Manners does not presume to know the tastes of your friends better than you. She is only suggesting that expanding the idea of what makes a suitable wedding or anniversary present is better than killing the practice of generosity.

The One-Year-To-Give-A-Present Rule

DEAR MISS MANNERS—My twenty-four-year-old son was recently in a wedding for his friend, and when I asked what he was giving the bridal couple, he told me that he hadn't even thought about it, since he had up to a year after the wedding to send a gift.

I guess my shock was apparent because he proceeded to tell me that this was the new social rule for gift-giving. He said that everyone his age knows that, and that the rules as I once knew them had changed.

GENTLE READER—You almost caught Miss Manners there. If she hadn't been paying strict attention, she might have acquiesced in your son's assertion that this was a new rule and obliged you by sliding into the things-are-deteriorating mode.

The fact is, though, that this is a very old rule. That it happens to be more sensible than ever in a time when marriages themselves may not last a year is coincidental. Any time from the announcement of the engagement until the end of the first year of marriage is considered appropriate for sending a wedding present.

Presents at a Reception

DEAR MISS MANNERS—Is it acceptable for an adult to attend a wedding and not bring a gift? I feel that it is not, but my fiancé says that you will say it is perfectly acceptable.

GENTLE READER—Oh, he does, does he? Funny, Miss Manners doesn't remember him from the Etiquette Council.

Having strenuously maintained that there is no social form, invitation, or announcement that translates as "Present due," Miss Manners might seem trapped into agreeing with your fiancé. Fortunately, she is wilier than that. If you do not feel sufficiently pleased by someone's marriage to be moved to try to contribute to that person's happiness, you don't belong at the wedding.

It is possible that your fiancé is referring to occasions where he accompanies you but does not actually know the bridal couple who are your friends. In that case, he may be included in your present. And Miss Manners trusts that you do not mean the verb "bring" literally. Wedding presents—properly sent to the bride's home before the wedding, or to the couple's home afterward—are a nuisance when brought to the event, where no one has time to deal with them and there is a danger of their being lost, the cards disappearing, or, Miss Manners regrets to say, the packages being stolen.

Not on the Registry

DEAR MISS MANNERS—I am puzzled and hurt, having just received a reproachful thank-you note from my stepsister. I chose a generous but not extravagant wedding gift that I thought she and her fiancé would enjoy and sent it with a card wishing them happiness. Her note informs me that they liked my gift, even if it wasn't on their bridal registry list.

I didn't realize that the bridal registry list had become the absolute ironclad means of choosing wedding gifts, and that imagination was no longer appreciated. What should I do the next time my stepsister and I meet? I don't want to allude to this incident, but I'm very much afraid she will.

GENTLE READER—It is indeed a topsy-turvy world where a guest is deemed thoughtless for making an effort to think of something that would be pleasing as a present and where a letter of thanks can be used to chide someone. This kind of thing drives Miss Manners to despair. Then she pulls herself together and agrees with your admirable stance that it is not worth a family quarrel. If your stepsister brings it up, you might allow yourself merely to murmur sincerely, "My intention was to please you."

Cash

DEAR MISS MANNERS—Is it true that a cash wedding gift these days should be at least one hundred dollars?

GENTLE READER—Who told you this? Some sweet little bride who could hardly stop blushing as she said it? Miss Manners doesn't approve of cash presents and only grudgingly admits them to the outer rim of propriety when people plead that they are bedridden, out of touch with the tastes of the recipients, or dealing with ingrates who spurn all other offerings. Even then, she can't help asking why one doesn't order by mail, or why one is anxious to please those one hardly knows or knows to be ungrateful. In any event, she will certainly be no party to establishing rates.

Presence Doesn't Count

DEAR MISS MANNERS—When attending a wedding abroad, what is considered proper for gift-giving, taking into account the guest's traveling expense to be in attendance? Can the guest's presence be considered as a gift?

GENTLE READER—Miss Manners is curious as to what you think your presence is worth. More than an electric can opener, but less than a tea service? Guests do not get expense accounts for attending weddings, which they can then apply against the debt of a wedding present.

Displaying the Presents

DEAR MISS MANNERS—When I was young (I am very old), it was the custom to spread out all the wedding presents for display at the bride's home, with the card of the donor beside the presents. No one does that now. When you suggest it, people are shocked.

It was fun. The guests used to walk around saying things like, "Oh, how pretty the crystal from Aunt Emma is" or "Uncle Louis' plates go so well with the table linens the Smiths gave, don't they?"

GENTLE READER—As partial as she is to tradition, Miss Manners, whose memory goes even farther back than yours, can think of many wedding customs that she would be leery of reviving. Don't ask about the others (they have to do with checking up on the bride's purity and the bridegroom's potency), but this is one.

In an age of consumerism, it would be unwise and unseemly to encourage people to evaluate and compare one another's wedding presents. Suffice it to say that Miss Manners doubts that the comments made would be confined to the sort of genteel compliments you recall.

13

GIVING AND RECEIVING THANKS

It has come to Miss Manners's attention that there is a great deal of misinformation circulating about thank-you notes. One such canard is that people who get married have up to a year to thank those who give them presents. This is a fiction perpetrated by brides with writer's cramp. No, they do not. Miss Manners gives them about twenty minutes after the arrival of each present; more lenient souls admit the possibility of its taking up to two weeks. The highly rude notion that one can wait a year to express thanks seems to have originated with the correct rule that one can send a wedding present within a year after the marriage. But once received, it must be acknowledged immediately.

Is Thanking Passé?

DEAR MISS MANNERS—Three months ago, I attended a wedding for a niece of mine and I have not received a thank-you for the gift I gave them. I was told by the mother of the bride that it is not necessary to send thank-you notes anymore. I have never heard of such a rude thing before.

GENTLE READER—A fatal problem with amateur etiquette advice-givers (especially those who should have recused themselves from the situation out of a glaring conflict of interest) is that they only do half the job.

If the writing of thank-you letters is to be declared defunct, then the giving of presents must also be declared defunct. You cannot have one without the other. Miss Manners suggests you stop giving these people presents and that you stop taking etiquette advice from them.

Dividing Tasks

DEAR MISS MANNERS—My husband and I decided to split the wedding gift thank-you-note duties into those of his friends and colleagues with whom I am not really acquainted, as his responsibility, and those of our mutual friends, my friends, and my parents' friends as my responsibility.

My notes went out promptly. Three months after the wedding, I realized he had only written a few notes, but he said he had verbally thanked just about everyone. I was mortified! I thought a note that long after the gift was given (we were married five months ago) would almost be insulting! To make matters worse, I just went over the list with him and he has only thanked a third of his colleagues. What on earth can I do? Is it too late to do anything?

GENTLE READER—It is late, but not too late, to write those thank-you letters; and it is exactly the right time now to work out a peaceful division of duties with your husband. The bargain you had made with him—that he write his circle and you write yours—is an eminently fair and reasonable one. However, insistence on always being fair in every little thing, as opposed to over the long run, is ruinous to the happiness of marriages.

The better way to divide things is that each of you takes over the tasks you don't mind doing and you either split the rest or decide that you both hate them so much that you will sacrifice elsewhere in order to be able to pay someone to do them. We can now take it as a given that your husband hates writing letters. His excuse—that he thanked people verbally—not only violates the rule of etiquette that wedding presents deserve letters, but also violates the bargain you made with him.

These letters must be written and it is a task you may not hire anyone else to do. Miss Manners assures you that it is more insulting to ignore a wedding present than it is to send a belated letter. So you should sit down this minute and write them, just as you managed to write those other letters.

Is this fair? Sure, if you say, "Okay, I'll be the letter writer in the family. But you know what I've always hated? Vacuuming. I can't stand it. You don't seem to mind—will you do all the vacuuming in the family?"

Deputizing the Task

DEAR MISS MANNERS—I attended a grand wedding in my daughter's husband's family and sent them a pair of silver candlesticks. After quite some time, I received a thank-you note. But the odd thing was that the note was not in the bride's handwriting, but in her mother's! I know her handwriting well and so does my daughter. There is no mistaking it. The note was written in the first person—"I," not "they"—throughout. Such as "Bob and I really love the silver candlesticks and they look so nice in our new home" signed with the daughter's new name.

Miss Manners, is this now an acceptable way of thanking someone for a wedding gift? To me, it almost borders on forgery. Nor does it do the daughter any favor, as she certainly isn't teaching the daughter the values of responsibility or honesty, do you think?

Dear Aunt Stacey and Uncle Trevor,

Darling Airhead gasped when we opened your box and saw the amazing brass elephant. What a unique idea. We both feel very comfortable with elephants and Darling is trying to decide whether it should be on the coffee table or on top of the bookcase. We hope you will come and see it —and us— once we get settled in our apartment. We're looking forward to seeing you at the wedding. Darling joins me in thanking you for such a handsome and generous present.

Darling sends her love with mine,

Orville

It doesn't matter whether the bride or the bridegroom writes the letters of thanks for wedding presents provided that these out immediately after the arrival of each present and are not in handwriting of the bride's mother. An expression of enthusiasm for the specific present is required, whether or not it is felt.

GENTLE READER—It seems to Miss Manners that your friend has long since taught her daughter something about responsibility: namely, that she can get her mother to do her job.

Thank-Yous for Money

DEAR MISS MANNERS—Over half of the wedding gifts we received were gifts of money. How would one go about writing a thank-you card to someone for such a gift without sounding crude?

GENTLE READER—However useful and welcome money may be, it is, Miss Manners would like to point out, a crude present. For one thing, the recipient knows exactly what it cost. The most graceful way to disguise this in your thanks is to select a real present on that person's behalf—that is, to tell the donor what you have bought with the money. The rest of the thanks can then apply to the present, as if the giver had selected it.

Thanking Oneself

DEAR MISS MANNERS—Since the majority of the '60s generation, especially brides, are slow with thank-you notes for gifts, could a self-addressed, stamped envelope with note paper be enclosed in the gift box? Brides enclose similar envelopes for R.s.v.p.'s.

GENTLE READER—Miss Manners sees that you are generously willing to forgo the give-and-take of present giving, by assigning the guest both the task of giving the present and thanking him- or herself for having done so. This doesn't seem quite fair. Perhaps such a bride ought to be allowed to buy herself a present and then thank herself or not as she prefers.

Prewritten Thanks

DEAR MISS MANNERS—At an extremely extravagant wedding I attended, there was a printed card at every place setting at the dinner table stating, "Thank you very much for sharing this special day with us, and thank you for your gift."

Am I behind the times (I am twenty-seven, and have been to many weddings but never came across this)? I thought a thank-you note was to be very personal, handwritten, and was to state the gift received.

GENTLE READER—Personal? Do you think of the relationship between bridal couple and their guests as personal, rather than commercial?

Evidently these people think otherwise. They have provided an all-purpose, standardized receipt which is not going to thrill those who had hoped to hear that whatever they had selected actually touched and pleased the couple. But Miss Manners can imagine that their method would be of advantage to those who had not selected a present and who can now forget about doing so, although honor would then require them to leave the card on the table.

Fishing for a Thank-You

DEAR MISS MANNERS—I left a wedding gift in the form of a check at a wedding I attended several months ago. I had met the bride once before, years ago, but had never met the groom. Thus far, I have not received any acknowledgment that my gift was received. It was cashed a month after the wedding, but I would like to know that it was received by the proper party. Is there any specific correct waiting time before making inquiries? I could call the bride's parents, but do not want to embarrass them or their daughter unless necessary.

GENTLE READER—You know and Miss Manners knows that what bothers you is not the presumption that the check was stolen and cashed with a forged signature, but the likelihood that these ingrates took your money and never bothered to thank you for it. To give a present to someone who doesn't even acknowledge it is galling. You shouldn't be ashamed to admit it—to admit it to Miss Manners, that is. You can't admit it to the ingrates or their relatives, because that would be a social declaration of war.

This brings us full circle back to your claim that you are merely afraid that your present went astray. Indeed, that is the excuse used to point out that a present was never acknowledged. Miss Manners doesn't know why she forced your real feelings out of you, except as ammunition against the rude, who are given to claiming, on no evidence whatsoever, that "no one cares about receiving thank-you notes any more."

In the case of a bought present, one voices doubts about the store where it was purchased, or the mail or delivery service, so as to avoid accusing the recipient. With checks it is harder, because you have evidence from your own bank that the check was received. By all means, question the parents (who seem to be the people you actually know) as to whether this is, indeed, their daughter's handwriting, with which you are not familiar. Let them figure out why you are not familiar with their daughter's handwriting, so they can pass the embarrassment on where it belongs.

14

THE
RECEPTION

The two styles of menus for wedding guests are Dainty and Heartburn. Dainty, which can be little more than finger sandwiches, wedding cake, and champagne or punch, is rather chic and a whole lot cheaper. Nevertheless Miss Manners does not advise administering this to families coming from one of the many traditions that consider that a wedding from which the guests don't reel away holding their bloated tummies does not constitute a real marriage.

Within those choices, the time of day is what counts. Are these people going to be starving? A morning or noon wedding is followed by a wedding breakfast, which in the inscrutable manner of etiquette means a luncheon. An afternoon wedding requires only teatime fare. The increasingly popular evening wedding does call for dinner, which makes it a poor choice for a limited budget.

The Long Wait

DEAR MISS MANNERS—At one wedding we attended, we waited for two hours at the reception and the bride and groom showed up as we were leaving. They were joyriding in their rented limousine. At another, we waited an hour and a half while pictures were taken. My mother (who was once kept waiting three hours at a wedding reception) told me that in her day, photos were taken a week in advance so that delays were avoided. We can't figure out what has changed.

GENTLE READER—What has changed is the concept that guests are guests. These people seem to think of them more as a background crowd, with nothing better to do than to stand around until there is something at which to gawk. The first couple preferred to entertain themselves, rather than their guests, and the second wedding was aimed at posterity, rather than those in attendance. That their victims don't retaliate by simply going home when they are ignored is a miracle of manners.

The Receiving Line

DEAR MISS MANNERS—I feel that a receiving line at the wedding ceremony or reception is unnecessary—that greeting the guests individually at the reception is more personal. Several of my coworkers believe that the traditional receiving line is mandatory for the 250 guests who will be attending our wedding.

GENTLE READER—Let's say that you got Miss Manners to agree with you. "All right," she would declare, "no receiving line, provided you make guarantees that the key figures of the wedding will all greet every single one of those 250 guests personally, making absolutely sure not to miss any."

How would this be managed? Well, the bride, bridegroom and at least some of the parents, as hosts, would all have to stand by the door to be sure to get everyone entering. Poof! You have reinvented the receiving line. Now perhaps you can tell Miss Manners why the very name of such a practical and hospitable institution frightens people.

The Receiving-Line Order

DEAR MISS MANNERS—My husband and I are giving my stepson a small wedding reception soon, and need your advice on receiving-line etiquette. Both the bride's parents and the groom's parents are divorced and are either remarried or seriously involved with another. The reception is small, only fifty to seventy-five people. It is formal, with candlelight dining. My husband is paying for most of the expenses. The bride's mother is also contributing. The bride's father and the groom's mother are not contributing to the occasion. In what order should the receiving line be?

GENTLE READER—In order of the size of their financial contributions, Miss Manners supposes you expect her to say. Deadbeats need not apply.

Well, money has nothing whatever to do with it. The custom is for either the mothers of the couple, or their mothers and fathers, to receive with the bridal couple. If you and the bridegroom's mother get along well, you might join them as hostess, but Miss Manners hopes you will not make an issue of it. There are too many extraneous people here, some of them not even related, and they will all be screaming to be treated "fairly."

However, you only asked about the order. If you really want to have a receiving line nearly as long as the guest list, Miss Manners will put her feelings aside and give you an order:

1. The bride's mother
2. The bridegroom's father
3. You
4. The bride's mother's husband
5. The bridegroom's mother
6. The bride's father

7. The bride's stepmother
8. The bride's stepfather

And oh, yes—then the bride, bridegroom, and bridesmaids.

Note that this is not "order of importance." The traditional idea is to mix up the two families (bride's mother, bridegroom's father, bridegroom's mother, bride's father). Miss Manners has merely added the rule, when families are mixed enough already, of avoiding juxtaposing people who used to be married to each other, or to each other's spouses. It makes far too interesting a spectacle for the guests.

The Cuisine

DEAR MISS MANNERS—Please help a young bride-to-be! My fiancé is Italian and I am Yugoslavian. He says he would like Italian food served at our reception. I do not want to make my side of the family feel left out by serving Italian dishes only, nor do I want a mishmash of international courses or dishes representing both sides. In fact, I do not want to make an ethnic statement at all with the food. I simply want something neutral (roast beef, for example) that just feeds everyone.

My fiancé will not agree to this compromise and claims his side will be offended. My family is willing to go with the Italian food, but I am not. This will only serve to have the meal slant the wedding to one culture. What is proper in such a situation?

GENTLE READER—In the New World, we don't consider eclectic menus to be "an international mishmash," but rather the interesting use of different traditions. This is especially appropriate when it is likely to flatter and please the guests, not to mention the bridegroom.

It has not escaped Miss Manners's attention that you are marrying into a family of Italian origin, as he is into a family of Yugoslavian origin. Casting out both traditions for the sake of fairness is a bad way to start a marriage. Hardly better is the notion that everything must be exactly equal. If both families felt strongly, you should try to please both in the menu. But if your family doesn't care, what possible reason is there not to please his?

The Menu

DEAR MISS MANNERS—We are planning a wedding dinner for fifty guests. The caterers offer three entrée choices, with selections to be made in advance. This plan would entail reponse cards listing choices, a seating chart, place cards, etc. It seems to me that we, as hosts, should simply decide on a single entrée as we would if the dinner were at our home.

GENTLE READER—Miss Manners shares whatever exasperation you may feel that people cannot simply sit down nowadays and eat—or not eat—whatever is put in front of them. They have to whine about it. There were always restrictions because of religion or allergies, long before people began scrutinizing their plates for philosophical or nutritional implications, but polite people accepted graciously what was offered, eating what they could and ignoring the rest.

Now home entertaining has had to alter slightly as a result of the society's preoccupation with what it eats—or food fussing, to use the technical term. A good host is by no means obliged to provide different meals-on-order for everyone, but tries to have a wide-ranging menu that will give at least some sustenance to everyone. Try to do the same for the wedding dinner. Miss Manners finds the project of having guests order in advance not only ridiculous and cumbersome, but ultimately futile, as no two or three choices could possibly accommodate all the variations now in common practice.

The Cash Bar

DEAR MISS MANNERS—Do you think it is appropriate to have a full or partial cash bar at a wedding reception? Some coworkers and I were wondering if it would be rude to ask your guests to pay for a drink, or whether today's economy warrants such actions.

GENTLE READER—Miss Manners is going to take to drink herself, if she keeps having to listen to that argument. No, you cannot use the economy as an excuse for the extreme rudeness of charging your own guests for their refreshment.

Have you never heard of the blessed poor who share what little they have, while vile and greedy people who begrudge sharing are accursed? If you can't afford liquor at your wedding reception, serve tea or punch. If you can't afford that, serve water. But serve it graciously.

For the Wedding Party Only

DEAR MISS MANNERS—A friend told me that at her wedding reception, she plans on having champagne for the wedding party only. I think it is rude and ill-mannered not to include everyone. I have suggested that since they cannot afford champagne for everyone, they shouldn't have it just for some. Instead, they should just have it for themselves after the reception is over. She says this has been done at other weddings (which should not justify it as being proper).

GENTLE READER—It sure doesn't. The perversions of hospitality being practiced at modern weddings would make your hair curl, Miss Manners trusts. However, this has got to be high among them. If one cannot afford something special for one's guests, one does not consume that very thing in front of them. Nor does one invite certain people and then demonstrate to them that they are second-class guests. Did the bridegroom have a part in this idea? If not, Miss Manners worries about him. If so, she only worries about their children.

In Which the Bride and the Bartender Fight over the Tips

DEAR MISS MANNERS—At a wedding reception where there is an "open bar," there is a large brandy snifter, vase, glass jar, whatever on the bar. Who is the money which is left by the guests meant for? I say it is a tip for the bartender. My daughter says the money is for the bride and groom. Please advise as to who is correct.

GENTLE READER—Nobody. Everybody here is so incorrect that Miss Manners feels like offering you all the change in the bottom of her purse just to go away. There is no correct use of a large brandy snifter on the bar at a wedding reception except for the convenience of a guest requesting brandy; the vase should be used for flowers, and the glass jar should have been thrown away once the maraschino cherries were used up. At a private function, it is not customary to tip the bartender, much less the bride.

The Seating Plans

DEAR MISS MANNERS—Why do brides take it upon themselves to arrange seating charts like a fourth-grade teacher?

Since their guests are presumed to be adults, can't they make their own decisions about whom to eat with?

I attended a cousin's wedding, halfway across the country. Although distance has prevented us from being close, my cousin is a wonderful person. A sizable contingent of my family was going, and since I am fond of them and do not often have the chance to see them, the opportunity seemed worth the airfare and hassles of travel. But at the reception, we were assigned tables for dinner and while most of my family sat at one table across the room, I ate with eight total strangers. (Since I am perceived as single, the invitation was for me only, and I did not bring my significant other.) While these people were all very pleasant, I would have preferred to spend time with my family.

Shortly after, I attended the wedding of a college friend. The invitation was again for one, and since my significant other did not know anyone from my college years and was not interested in going, he stayed home. It did not seem worth it, or even proper, to make an issue of it. The guests fell into two categories: dear friends I haven't seen in some time and people I had hoped never to see again in my life. Again we were assigned tables and you can guess where I was assigned. Granted that the meals only last an hour or so. But when you've traveled a great distance to see people you haven't seen in years, time is more valuable.

GENTLE READER—The reason that adults can't find their own seats at a wedding is that they turn childish and start turning over chairs to save seats, arguing about where they want to be, feeling no responsibility for wallflowers, and so on. For a formal meal, seating should be worked out in advance.

But these brides were operating on the assumption that the only social desire of single people is to meet other single people. While weddings are traditional sources of other weddings, such is not always the case. Weddings also function as family reunions and this should be taken into account. Alternating family seating groups with ones including strangers likely to be of interest romantically or socially is a sensible compromise.

The Toasts

DEAR MISS MANNERS—When our daughter got married, a strain developed between the groom's parents and ourselves. They chose not to speak at the rehearsal dinner or the wedding. I'm sure no one has to speak about their son or daughter, but isn't it strange?

GENTLE READER—As these people are now your daughter's parents-in-law, Miss Manners urges you to put the omission down to an oversight or stage fright and relieve that strain. Only if you promise to do so will she tell you, for the record, that yes, if the bridegroom's parents give the rehearsal dinner, his father (or mother) should welcome the guests with the first toast, to be returned by the bride's father, after which anybody who is so moved, sober, or brief may offer one. At the wedding itself, the best man offers the first toast, and others may follow, including the bridegroom, to offer toasts to his bride and to her parents.

Businesslike Guests

DEAR MISS MANNERS—During our wedding reception, a number of friends mentioned to us that the wife of one of my best friends was passing out bright (orange with black print) flyers for her new house-cleaning business. (Our wedding colors were orchid and black.) At the time, I did not know what to say or do, so we did nothing. Should I have said something to her at the time, or is it too late to say something now? Was this proper?

GENTLE READER—Please don't give Miss Manners false clues, however entertaining. For one awful moment, she thought your objection might be that the flyers clashed with your color scheme.

It would have been preferable to stop this outrage when it occurred, although Miss Manners sympathizes with your paralysis at the idea of reprimanding a wedding guest. It would have been best to send an usher to collect the flyers and hand them back to the offender with the explanation, "This is not a business occasion."

Now it seems pointless to make a fuss, unless you plan to take the unwise step of inviting this person to another party. In that case you could say, when you issue the invitation, "This will be a social occasion, at which we prefer that business not be conducted." Better yet, you can have great fun turning the wedding anecdote into the kind of you'll-never-believe-this story that gets funnier, Miss Manners promises you, as time goes by.

Loud Music

DEAR MISS MANNERS—When attending a wedding reception and sitting with friends or family one may not have seen for some time, it would be most enjoyable to concentrate more on companionship than the loud band. As the volume goes up louder and louder, it becomes impossible to hear what the person next to you is saying. One must leave the table and find a quieter spot to catch up. Would it be rude to ask that the volume not be so loud? Or is this standard at wedding receptions? Very inconsiderate.

GENTLE READER—Yes, it is—inconsiderate, standard, and loud. But before you take that as Miss Manners's encouragement to stop the wedding by saying, "Will you kids please quiet down; some of us are trying to talk!" she must ask how you plan to make your request. You cannot, of course, disturb the wedding and you cannot step in and manage it. What you can do is to take one of the hosts aside—make that the parent with whom you are connected—and ask plaintively, "Is there somewhere the guests at my table can go to talk? We don't want to bother anyone, but we can't hear ourselves over the music."

Doggie Bags

DEAR MISS MANNERS—Over the past year, my family and I have attended a few weddings and we hope you can tell us what would be the proper etiquette technique when there are plenty of leftovers from the sweet table at a reception. I say to eat what you want and take home any leftovers, knowing that it would be a waste of food if it's not eaten. My family says to eat what you want and leave the leftovers alone, or bring home any leftover pastries only if they are served at each table and the bride and groom don't mind that you take them.

GENTLE READER—What did you have in mind here? Tapping the bridal couple on the shoulders during their last dance and asking them if you could run off with their food? Miss Manners gathers that your plans involve more than taking home two bites of wedding cake to put under your pillow so that you can dream of your future spouse. Is going off with two or three layers of uneaten cake more like what you were considering?

It is kind of you to worry about food waste, but that happens to be the problem of the hosts. Perhaps they have plans for it. Perhaps, unless you plan to outlast them, not everyone will be finished eating by the time you decide that there is enough to sustain you later. Miss Manners has defended the practice of the so-called doggie bag at restaurants, but the case is different; there, the diner has purchased the food. Guests are offered refreshment at an event, not a share of the investment for future use.

Staying On

DEAR MISS MANNERS—My daughter and her fiancé have invited many out-of-town friends whom they haven't seen for a few years, and they want to stay at their wedding reception until it is over. Her grandmother says they should leave at a reasonable hour and not make the guests stay.

If they throw the bouquet, etc., and then leave to get changed, I feel they can return and party with their friends. We want people to stay as long as they wish, but not to feel they must stay if they want to leave. Would it be appropriate for the Master of Ceremonies to make an announcement to this effect?

GENTLE READER—The fact that newlyweds feel cheated if they have to go off and spend the evening alone has become increasingly, not to mention indecorously, apparent in recent years. As a result, the rule about guests not leaving until the bridal couple does is routinely violated and the couple does eventually end up alone, although at the reception site itself.

Miss Manners prefers your solution of the formal, but not actual, departure to the one about announcing that people are free to leave. Of course they are, but being told so, however merciful the motivation, can only make them think that they have long overstayed their welcome.

The Aftermath

DEAR MISS MANNERS—My sister is having a full wedding (the couple has lived together for a few years) and all of the immediate family is traveling from out of town. The couple has not offered to help with expenses. They say they have to

pay for the wedding. Most of the family is returning immediately after the wedding and my sister is upset that no one
is staying over an extra day to watch her open her gifts. Is
this a new tradition—watching the bride open gifts?

GENTLE READER—How old is this bride? She seems to be
confusing the tradition of the single-digit birthday party
with her wedding. Watching people open presents, unless it
is the joking offerings of a rare adult birthday party, is not a
grown-up occupation.

The new tradition here, if you want to call it that, is the
marathon wedding. Although a party the night before the
wedding has long been customary, next day parties featuring the bridal couple did not appear until everyone was
willing to admit that the newlyweds had no particular reason to want to be alone together.

A guest's obligation when attending a wedding is still
only for the ceremony and celebration immediately following. If others want to hang around longer, out of sentiment,
curiosity about the wedding presents, or cheaper air fares if
they stay over, it is fine to plan events to entertain them. But
guests are not obliged to stay after the wedding day to witness the marriage.

15

THE CANCELED WEDDING

Should the whole thing seem to be more trouble than it is worth, the wedding is called off with no more illuminating explanation than a dignified, "It was a mutual decision—we have the highest esteem for each other." If formal invitations have been issued, they must be formally recalled:

> *Mr. and Mrs. Greatly Relieved*
> *announce that the marriage of their daughter*
> *Darling Airhead*
> *to Mr. Fortune Hunter*
> *will not take place*

If wedding announcements have been engraved or printed, thrifty Miss Manners suggests you make use of them by correcting them with a pen so that they read:

> *Mr. and Mrs. Greatly Relieved*
> *have the honour of announcing*
> *that the marriage of their daughter*
> *Darling Airhead*
> *to*
> *Mr. Fortune Hunter*
> *will not take place*

The Response to a Canceled Wedding

DEAR MISS MANNERS—Could you please advise this gentle reader on the appropriate response one should make to receiving an announcement of a wedding being canceled? The wedding had been planned for years, was to be very large and formal, and was canceled one week before the date. There was a formally printed announcement mailed out.

It seems that some response on the part of the recipient is warranted; however, this seems like a land mine for etiquette errors. If one calls the bride, it may put her in an awkward position of feeling that she has to offer some sort of explanation. To not respond in some way seems cold and uncaring.

GENTLE READER—It is indeed an etiquette land mine that you describe and Miss Manners is always grateful to those who chart new territory for her. The least she can do is to help you find your way back.

At least one of the parties involved—erstwhile bride, bridegroom, or a parent—is a friend of yours. Rather than placing a call, which you astutely realize might be awkward, dash off a note to your friend saying "I wish you (or Natasha or Calvin) all the best, and would love to see you." A reintroduction to normal social life, with no explanations required, would doubtless be welcome.

The Broken Engagement

DEAR MISS MANNERS—I'm in love with the man I was once engaged to. Our plans were put on hold because he had a problem that arose from the past with his ex-girlfriend and resulted in marriage. We are still seeing each other and very much in love. He wants out, but due to his financial situation, he's not stable enough to move out at this time. But he is in the process of taking care of this financial problem.

To me, it's taking a long time. It's been eight months and there are no children involved. Just recently, we decided not to see each other until he's out of this situation because several of our plans were canceled due to this. We call from time to time, keeping communication. I'm only going to give him one and a half months to take care of this, but I did not tell him that.

GENTLE READER—A man who persuaded his fiancée that he loves her but has had to solve a little problem by temporarily marrying someone else may well have broken some etiquette rules. It's just difficult for Miss Manners to find the shards in all that moral debris.

If the question now is whether you are breaking any by rescuing yourself, the answer is no. One can hardly dissolve an engagement more thoroughly than he did, so you have been relieved of any obligations.

Returning the Ring

DEAR MISS MANNERS—My son received money from my husband and me for graduation from college and used it for an engagement ring for his fiancée. Several months later, she did some things to hurt him, so he called off the engagement, four months before the wedding date. Being a spoiled rich girl, the fiancée had put her wedding invitations on "rush order" in hopes he would change his mind when the invitations were received.

To make a long story short, they have not reconciled and he says they never will get married. He has asked her for the ring back, but she said her mother told her to keep it, as it is the least my son could do after all the expense to her family in preparation for the wedding.

GENTLE READER—Miss Manners is afraid that it never occurred to etiquette to pass a rule against rushing the wedding invitations in a desperate attempt to hoodwink a reluctant bridegroom. But it strikes her as rather a nasty idea to invite innocent people to a doomed wedding, so she is willing to issue the rule now.

There certainly is a rule that a lady whose engagement is broken returns the ring. This was found necessary precisely to counter that unpleasant urge to grab whatever assets are at hand, so to speak, and to encourage jilted ladies to maintain the more acceptable posture of scorning a token from someone who has proven unworthy. Unfortunately, etiquette does not have a police force to send in to enforce this. Should the gentleman wish to pursue the matter, you must consult the less subtle form of encouraging polite behavior known as the law.

Keeping the Wedding Presents

DEAR MISS MANNERS—I have always understood that when a wedding does not take place as planned, wedding and shower gifts are returned. But what if the wedding is called off and yet the couple sets up housekeeping together anyway?

In the case I know, the presents were kept and seem to be regarded by the couple as housewarming gifts for the new house that they have bought. I have received a thank-you letter telling me how nice my gift looks in their home and assuring me that they appreciate my kindness as they "embark on their new life together."

Frankly, my idea of a housewarming gift is a bottle of wine, not the silver and china that we were asked to select from the bride-to-be's register at a local store. I know I sound like a prude or a tightwad, but this seems wrong to me.

GENTLE READER—Miss Manners isn't crazy about it, either. Wedding presents should be returned if a wedding is called off. She presumes that the couple's not-very-nice rationale is that the engagement was not exactly broken. Rather, the clock has been turned back to a preengagement state of courtship which may or may not progress to a wedding. If it does, send them a lot of good wishes unaccompanied by a package.

16

EQUIVALENTS AND ENCORES

Two Weddings

DEAR MISS MANNERS—A young couple who lived together for a year and then were married in a civil ceremony at the courthouse have just—six months later—issued invitations to a large, formal church wedding and all of the additional traditional accompaniments—rehearsal dinner, reception at the country club, etc. They are being advised and encouraged by their parents, who should know better. I am only a friend, but it hurts to hear the critical, and sometimes cruel, comments being made about this plan. Many people treat it as a joke, or say it is just a way to get the presents not received after the private civil ceremony. Are two such weddings proper? It seems odd to me. Perhaps I am way behind the times.

GENTLE READER—Miss Manners, too, finds it is extremely odd that the wedding, as a social event, has become increasingly divorced, if one may use that term, from the actual marriage ceremony. What your friends did is not unique. Weddings are commonly being held now for already-married couples, with various explanations. If it is during the first year, they say that the necessity of having the actual ceremony earlier (more usually for reasons of taxes than pregnancy, which seems to be no longer in the urgent category) didn't give them time to plan the party. If it is even longer after that, they say that the original wedding wasn't the wedding of their dreams, or, if it was, that they want to renew this dream.

Miss Manners can understand the ceremonial yearning, if you will. But the idea of satisfying it totally aside from the reality of the sacred and legal union at the heart of it gives the couple a sort of unpleasant air of entitlement. Surely, the sentiment connected with the real exchange of vows ought to be powerful enough to remain unique, however simply it was done, and whatever festive parties are later given in celebration of it.

In other words, there is nothing wrong with a newly married couple giving a later reception or dinner, however formal they wish it to be, or for a couple married longer to have a fancy anniversary party. Of course they want to celebrate their marriage with family and friends in an elaborate way.

When guests find that they have been invited to a wedding that turns out to be only a reenactment, they do feel that some sort of fraud is being perpetrated. Mind you, Miss Manners does not approve of such carping. Those who are fond of the couple should participate in what is offered and those who are not should politely decline. But she does understand why they do not feel the same solemnity that they do about witnessing two people actually joining themselves in marriage.

Gay Wedding Etiquette

DEAR MISS MANNERS—My wife and I have been invited to the Episcopal commitment ceremony of a male couple. I work with one of the gentlemen and my wife and I have entertained the couple many times over the years. We are honored to witness the union of these fine people, but are unsure of the etiquette surrounding a same-sex ceremony. Specifically, are gifts expected? Where does one sit? Are grade-school-age children permitted? My wife suggests that when in doubt, we defer to the etiquette of traditional weddings. Is this advised?

GENTLE READER—As this ceremony is intended to simulate a wedding, you would do well to follow your wife's suggestion of following the etiquette observed at weddings. Since weddings are public ceremonies, the first rule is not to get too interested in the sexual angle. So stop worrying about which is the bride's side and which the bridegroom's. Besides, as you are friends of both, it wouldn't matter. Sit where an usher indicates or where you find places.

One should never bring uninvited guests anywhere. If your children were not invited, they should not attend, no matter what their age. No one is ever supposed to expect presents, although Miss Manners has heard enough of such expectations to last a lifetime. But as these people are your friends, she imagines you will want to send them something to commemorate the occasion.

The Mock Wedding

DEAR MISS MANNERS—My daughter and her fiancé are planning a public "ceremony" with family and close friends in attendance, at which time they will share their vows of love and commitment for one another. They do not plan to legally wed.

What is the procedure in this situation—how is the announcement/invitation worded? Are showers/gifts appropriate? I am totally in the dark on this one. Any light you can shed would be gratefully received.

The pleasure of the company of

The Honorable John Adams and Mr. David Bart

is requested at the commitment ceremony of

Mr. Gregory Awful

and

Mr. Lars Uhmm

on Saturday, the eleventh of November

at half after four o'clock

6 Victoria Walk

Brookdale-by-the-Sea, Connecticut

The favour of a reply is requested

Although this is not actually a wedding invitation, it follows an optional but particularly flattering traditional form, in which the guests' names are written by hand.

GENTLE READER—Goodness gracious, if these people haven't gone and reinvented the mock wedding! Miss Manners has always said that if you live long enough, you will see everything come back into fashion, no matter how foolish.

The mock wedding was a staple of nineteenth-century melodrama, although its antecedents are more ancient. Traditionally, it was planned by the bridegroom, with the aid of some rascally friends, in order to delude the bride into thinking she had been legally wed. The custom was for the bridegroom to point out to her shortly afterward— sometimes the next morning—that she was not and to bid her adieu. Showers, gifts, invitations, and announcements were all unnecessary.

When the bride is in on the planning, as in this case, the mock wedding seems to lose its point. Why simulate a wedding in order to have two people announce in public that they are in love? Can't they just carve their initials on a tree like everyone else?

The Repeat Wedding

There seem to be an increasing number of people around who want to have second weddings without all the fuss and expense of divorce. So they are staging repeat weddings, in which, as long-married couples, they "renew" or "reaffirm" their wedding vows, with varying amounts of bridal trimming.

Considering the state of marriage nowadays, Miss Manners would like to congratulate these couples. She would also like to inject a note of caution about their desire to elicit more than congratulations from their friends.

An established married couple should not lightly ask others to shower them with bridal honors—as opposed simply to attending an anniversary party—just because they have lived happily ever after. That is, after all, what they promised to do the first time.

It may not seem fair that those who stage repeated weddings with different partners have glutted the market, but the patience of potential wedding guests has been sorely tried. At the very least, a repeat wedding should be a decent interval after the original one—preferably measured in quarters of centuries.

The rule about inviting people to wedding renewals is the opposite of that for first weddings: At first weddings, the more elaborate the arrangements, the more people you can invite. At repeats, one's entire circle of friends can be invited to a party given after the simple participation in a religious service, or during which the vows are just spoken, almost as if the couple were toasting each other.

If there is to be a serious restaging, only people who are very closely and dearly attached to the couple, such as their descendants, the original bridal party, and really intimate friends, should be expected to think them charming in their original wedding clothes—or the outfits they had always wanted but couldn't afford when they were young.

This brings Miss Manners to the motivation for restaging a wedding, when one can have all the festivities of a celebration without the ceremonial repetition. She supposes that the most endearing reason for wanting a repeat wedding is to act on the lovely sentiment of "I'd marry you all over again today." After all, most people married that long were married in an era when one had to take a leap of faith without knowing the other person's daily household habits. Another reason may be that a couple had omitted the religious ceremony, which they now want to celebrate. Miss Manners can also imagine that couples whose wedding vows got damaged and then repaired might crave a formal fresh start.

Miss Manners is aware that she antagonizes people by

her lack of enthusiasm for the newly popular renewal-of-vows ceremonies, in a time when congratulations seem in order for every week that a married couple actually manages to stay married. But however often wedding vows are broken, they are still serious vows, made for the length of life itself. They are not limited business contracts, with options to renew every year. To remake an eternal vow after only one year seems to make a joke out of the permanence that the marriage vow states.

Miss Manners should not have to caution decent people that one does not have a repeat wedding as a fund-raising drive for one's favorite cause—such as a trip one could not otherwise afford to take, or a pension to continue the marriage. She does have to warn those who are properly horrified that the event might be taken for such that there is only one correct way to head off making guests feel obligated to send presents for an announced repeat wedding or anniversary party and that is to issue party invitations—formal or informal—without telling people in advance what the occasion is. They will be pleasantly surprised when they get there, and will keep murmuring, "I wish I'd known—I would have liked to get you something," but that is not to be taken literally.

The Fifty-Year-Old Wedding

DEAR MISS MANNERS—My parents did not have a traditional wedding, since they eloped, and therefore my mother wants as many of the trappings of a regular wedding as she can get for their fiftieth wedding anniversary. Their plans include having six of the youngest grandchildren (age four to twelve) walk up the aisle, dressed in coordinating, but not matching, outfits. She'd like my sister, my brother and me walking up the aisle in procession, but I felt that our position in the front pew and participating in a reading during the Mass would be more appropriate. When she started talking about whether her original maid of honor or I, as elder daughter, should "stand for her" I began to think this has gone too far. My dad has just asked my brother to "stand for him" as his original best man is deceased.

I understand my mother's motivation, but I'd like to know how one draws the line in good taste between what's appropriate for a Golden Anniversary and what's just plain silly—as is my mother's hinting at wearing a veil. I don't want to begrudge my parents their legitimate cause to celebrate, but even my father has begun to wonder what is appropriate here.

GENTLE READER—After many years in this trade, Miss Manners is only now beginning to realize the hold the ritual of the formal wedding has over the American female imagination. Rather than being merely one ceremonial choice among many proper and traditional choices of styles in which to be married, the formal wedding is thought of, obsessively, as an entitlement. Not only do those who were unable to be married formally seem to count this as a permanent lack in their lives, but those who made another deliberate choice—who eloped or married informally because that is what they wanted at the time—also feel that the world owes them a formal wedding.

So here we have your mother, after fifty years of successful marriage, out to collect her place in a ritual to which she believes every lady who marries is entitled. And she is far from alone in this yearning. Superfluous wedding ceremonies on the part of people who are already married are becoming astonishingly common.

The formal wedding ceremony presupposed a young lady, shyly veiled and surrounded by her girlhood friends, going from her father's household to her bridegroom's. While we retain an affection for these forms, to make them

The Recessional

This bridegroom is happy not only because he is in love but also because he was not required to conscript extra ushers so that the recessional would look like a mass wedding. The flower girl was told to sit quietly with her parents after the processional, but her jumping back in, drunk with attention, has been greeted with fond amusement by the guests. Being more mature than she, they realize that a wedding is not entertainment and therefore have refrained from applauding during or after the ceremony.

The Receiving Line — Informal Wedding

Proper Remarks — (L to R)

[*To bride's mother*] "What a lovely wedding." [*To bridegroom's mother*] "What a lovely wedding." [*To bride*] "I wish you great happiness. You're such a beautiful bride!" [*To bridegroom*] "Congratulations! You're a lucky man." [*To matron of honor*] "What a beautiful wedding. And you look lovely.

All responses to remarks above are, "Thank you— I'm so glad you could be here."

apply to obviously independent ladies, there is such a thing as stretching it too far.

Like you, Miss Manners finds your mother's hopes slightly ridiculous. The bathos of a respectable older lady publicly revealing her dream of appearing as a young bride, is bound to seem foolish, however touching it may also be.

There is, then, a trade-off between pleasing your mother and subjecting her to ridicule. The family should try to gauge whether this event will be taken in a sympathetic spirit by those whom they propose to invite. Meanwhile, Miss Manners is thinking of revoking new couples' freedom to declare that they don't want any wedding fuss and to be married without such trappings. It creates too much trouble for the rest of us later on down the line. Then, too, people who underwent elaborate weddings seem to have acquired some sense of proportion about it all: Many of them claim that they wished they had eloped.

INDEX